Where
Colleges
Fail

By NEVITT SANFORD

(As author, co-author, editor)

WHERE COLLEGES FAIL

SELF AND SOCIETY

COLLEGE AND CHARACTER

THE AMERICAN COLLEGE

THE AUTHORITARIAN PERSONALITY

PHYSIQUE, PERSONALITY, AND SCHOLARSHIP

ALCOHOL PROBLEMS AND PUBLIC POLICY
(In press)

Where Colleges Fail

A Study of the Student as a Person

By
Nevitt
Sanford

Jossey-Bass Inc., Publishers

615 Montgomery Street · San Francisco · 1967

WHERE COLLEGES FAIL
A Study of the Student as a Person

by Nevitt Sanford

Copyright © 1967 by Jossey-Bass, Inc., Publishers

Copyright under Pan American and
Universal Copyright Conventions

Jossey-Bass, Inc., Publishers
615 Montgomery Street
San Francisco, California 94111

Library of Congress Catalog
Card Number 67–13279

Printed in the United States of America
by York Composition Company, Inc.
York, Pennsylvania

6723

2 3,539

FIRST PRINTING: *March 1967*
SECOND PRINTING: *July 1967*

THE JOSSEY-BASS SERIES IN HIGHER EDUCATION

General Editors

JOSEPH AXELROD, *San Francisco State College*

MERVIN B. FREEDMAN, *San Francisco State College*

Introduction

Only a few years ago, in *The American College,* I expressed the hope that public criticism of our colleges might induce the scholars and research men who run them to institute some reforms. It never occurred to me that students would organize protests against the kind of education they were receiving or that leading citizens would join the academic establishment in support of the old ways of doing things. What is most depressing about the statements of politicians and the irate letters to the editor that have followed student demonstrations is not their conservatism or their impatience with the younger generation, but the narrow way they conceive of education. In the minds of many citizens, "getting an education" seems to be a matter of acquiring units of information, measured mainly by the number of hours spent in the classroom. There is seldom a suggestion that college might help to change the individual himself, to broaden his horizons, to liberate him from dogma and prejudice, or to give him a new sense of identity. These changes do occur in colleges, however, especially where education is seen as a total experience embracing not only courses and examinations but opportunities for students to try various styles of life, to learn from each other, to have their un-examined belief-systems challenged, and, above all, to have associations with men who show in their lives the values of liberal education.

The prevalence of the narrow view of education is a reminder of how long teaching has been neglected in our institutions of higher learning, of how dominant and enduring are the academic structures of disciplines and courses that were designed less for the purpose of teaching than for the production of knowledge. It is ironical that leading citizens should share the prevailing, purely academic view of education when they have nothing to gain by it and when it stands in opposition to many of their own values and aspirations. Ask a state legislator, for example, in serious discussion what *he* got out of college and the chances are good that—after wryly commenting that he probably would not have got in under present admissions standards—he will recall a relationship with a professor, or something that he learned from his roommates and friends, or an experience on the athletic field, or his participation in the student protest of his day. Ask what he hopes college will do for his own son or daughter, beyond giving some preparation for a job, and he will mention personal qualities that he would like to see developed: independence of thinking, a sense of social responsibility, a capacity to judge people, the resourcefulness necessary to avoid boredom, and so on. Such an answer would suggest that the great humanistic purpose of education, though suppressed or put aside, has not been forgotten in our society; and that a college able to re-state this purpose, and show by its actions a rededication to it, would not only win the loyalty of its students, but also suffer no lack of constituents or supporters in the larger society.

My aim in *Where Colleges Fail* is to help restore the student to his rightful place at the center of the college's activities. I state the case for individual development as the primary aim of education, present a theory of how students actually develop, and then apply it to various aspects of the student's development and the college's educational procedures. Finally, I suggest ways in which colleges might take advantage of outside pressures instead of merely submitting to or ignoring them.

In arguing for individual development as the primary aim of education, I consider that I am largely restating in contemporary terms the philosophy of humanistic education that has persisted in Western civilization ever since the Greeks conceived the idea of *paideia*. It is the philosophy that inspired the British university colleges, was embraced by our Founding Fathers, and eloquently restated by President Truman's Commission on Education. It is still boldly stated in college catalogues and commencement addresses, even though it tends to be ignored in practice as students are increasingly abandoned in favor of specialized scholarship and often trivial research. I argue that there is a critical need for a reaffirmation of this philosophy, for it is only through individual development that a person can maintain his humanity and become truly useful in our technological, post-capitalistic society.

If the development of the individual as a whole is the primary aim, then colleges should organize all their resources in efforts to achieve it. Such planning of a *total* educational environment must be guided by a theory of personality—a theory in the terms of which it is possible to state specific goals for the individual, describe the interrelations of his various psychological processes, and understand the ways in which he changes under the impact of environmental influences.

According to the theory outlined in Part II the individual functions as a "system"; his various aspects develop in interaction with one another and developmental change occurs through challenge and self-knowledge. This theory, like the educational philosophy stated above, holds in a general way for people of any age. Thus, in discussing the processes of developmental change, I use observations of children and adolescents as well as of college students, and in Chapter 17 I apply the theory in a consideration of development in the years after college. Development is progressive and continuous. What is possible at a given educational level depends on the developmental stage that the students have reached, and the understanding of an individual requires that he be viewed in the context of all that has gone before in his life, as well as with attention to the direction in which he is headed. I hope, therefore, that this book will be of use not only to college educators but to those who have responsibility for, or interest in, young people who are soon to enter or have recently left college—and to the students themselves.

In applying my theory to various aspects of student development—social responsibility, motivation for academic achievement, creativity, and the integration of sex and of drinking within the personality—I have tried to show something of the intricate interactions of the cognitive and the emotional or characterological, and I argue that both must be considered in any educational endeavor. This may help lay to rest the false and troublesome dichotomy between "the intellective" which is often said to be the sole concern of educators, and "the non-intellective," *i.e.*, the rest of the personality, which is said to be the province of psychiatry or mental hygiene. The development—or the erosion—of virtues such as those just listed depends heavily on what happens in the classroom, even on the learning of content, but it also depends on various other experiences—some of which a college can deliberately provide. In order to make this point more sharply I have included chapters on sex and on drinking. The fact that these topics are important is no reason why they should be excluded from the college curriculum! I argue that topics that concern students deeply must be made objects of intellectual analysis. This can provide excellent training in the use of intelligence; and more than that, the awareness and control of feelings that may thus be attained are favorable to personality development in general.

In discussing some aspects of student development, in Part III, I consider the influences, favorable or unfavorable, of various features of the college environment. In Part IV I focus upon several particular aspects of the environment itself—student peer culture, teaching, the size of the institution—asking how they affect the student and how they might better serve his development. Here, too, I am concerned with wholeness—with the interrelations of various environmental influences and with how they combine in making their impact on students.

The outside pressures on colleges and universities that I discuss in the final Part are chiefly demands for expanded educational opportunities, and for knowledge and action relevant to the problems of our society. These demands are undoubtedly burdensome, in the short run, for some institutions, but by forcing abandonment of traditional ways they provide opportunities for constructive innovation. It is hard to see why any educator, in a democracy, should not take heart from the fact that more and more young people want the benefits of higher education, or why any university man should not be encouraged by the fact that citizens in increasing numbers expect wisdom and leadership, as well as knowledge of facts, from his institution. My argument, in Part V, is that universities or colleges that make student development their primary aim can find ways to integrate their activities and thus to serve society and students at the same time; for example, by combining science and practice (while themselves deciding what the problems are), and scholarship with involvement in the issues of our times, they may serve society directly; and then by arranging for the participation of students in these activities, as teachers as well as learners, as doers as well as hearers, they may best promote their development.

This book is based mainly on lectures and addresses given since the publication of *The American College* (1962). The general approach here is much the same as in my contributions to that volume, except that I now write about educational aims and needed reforms with a greater sense of urgency than before, and in restating my theoretical position I include only what seems essential and address myself to the general reader. In other respects the two books are hardly comparable. *The American College,* a product of 28 authors of various backgrounds, interests, and theoretical persuasions, is comprehensive, detailed, and eclectic; *Where Colleges Fail* addresses itself to aspects of student development and certain features of the college environment—mainly topics not discussed systematically in *The American College*—all of which are seen from the same point of view. In writing this book I have had the benefits of criticism of *The American College,* of observations and discussions at numerous colleges throughout the country, and of research on students at Stanford and Berkeley in the 1960s added to similar research at Vassar College in the 1950s.

Table of Contents

PART IV: THE EDUCATIONAL ENVIRONMENT

PART V: LINKS WITH THE LARGER SOCIETY

Where
Colleges
Fail

I

Educational
Goals and
Today's Students

1

The Education Needed Today

In the face of increasing enrollments, expanding knowledge, and climbing expenses, schools and colleges are less eager to question what they are doing than simply to find ways to do more of it. A mere enlargement of the system, however, will not suffice to meet the educational challenges being posed by changes in technology, in politics, and in society. After finding room for the student at college, we must ask what kind of world he will later inhabit, what it will demand of him, and how we can prepare him for it.

In the world of work, automation is transforming or eliminating occupational roles, with jobs at the unskilled and technical levels being affected first. As industry calls for new skills, vast retraining programs prepare men for new jobs which, in turn, are soon altered, thus starting a new cycle. Even in the professions, few are doing only what they were trained to do: in industry or science or service the most productive men are those who have done the most learning on the job, sometimes crossing traditional boundaries in the process. While the academic departments struggle to maintain their sovereignty, great advances are made in the no man's land between fields—

by physicists, for example, in genetics. As occupational roles shift or lapse altogether, and others appear, colleges are no longer able to train a student for his whole career, but only for its initial phase. The course of events is forcing recognition that, as liberal educators have long argued, we should seek to develop people as individuals instead of trying to train them for particular roles in society. We can provide adaptable intellectual tools, teach ways of approaching problems that are so general and so fundamental that they will serve in a great diversity of situations, and develop in students the flexibility which will enable them to go on learning and to maintain a stable sense of themselves through a succession of changing roles.

In our highly organized world, the student needs a broad education not only to keep pace with change but also to resist the pressures of specialization—pressures that now begin earlier than ever. Segregation according to age, sex, even personality is dictated by the requirements of the work that people are going to do. In our highly complex systems of business and government, even of professional and academic life, each role is meshed with so many others that any individuality—any personality, one might say—is like "noise" in a communication system. Even Ph.D.s in vast knowledge-producing organizations are virtually "programmed," much like the high-speed computers they use. Some organizations have even sought to guide the private lives of their employees, by hints and suggestions if not by rules.

If a person involved in this vast machinery is to find satisfaction in his work, he must have the breadth to see his productive role in perspective. If he is to maintain his personality, he must be able to see himself as existing independently of the organization; he must have something inside himself that will support his values against organizational pressures; and he must have an education general enough so that he can lead a meaningful life apart from his occupation. He may, for instance, learn to take more satisfaction in other social roles. Women have long been called upon to do such a diversity of things that to speak of educating them for a particular social role made little sense; accordingly, there has been more acceptance of a general liberal-arts education for them. But the situation is increasingly the same for men. A man can no longer define himself just in terms of his occupational role. He is also a father, an educator, a committee-man, a citizen, and probably, if he is in the middle class, an all-around do-it-yourself man. If he is to take these different roles comfortably, without feeling that his status is being lowered or his masculinity impaired, he must have a flexible self-conception based on familiarity with many aspects of his own personality.

The truth is that the whole meaning of work is changing. It is increasingly difficult for a man to make his vocational role the primary basis of self-respect or to teach his son the traditional values with respect to work. Having grown up in a society which raised hard work to the status of a moral virtue, he now must learn how to play; and in this sphere a liberal-arts education can show him the pleasure of using his mind in a way more broad and speculative than his work may call for. Such education can also further his physical and aesthetic development and refine his tastes as a consumer.

As the standard of living goes up, the role of consumer becomes more central in people's lives. What they choose to consume will determine the level of taste in our culture. If it is to be enhanced or even maintained, higher education must produce increasing numbers of sensitive and discriminating persons. Nothing refines our gross national product more surely than a growing and appreciative market for new creations by the talented. Schools and colleges must nurture this talent and enlarge the market for what it offers, especially the market for goods and services unavailable from machines.

Most important, education can help to restore the responsible individual, who is vanishing into a tangle of organized social roles and group memberships. It used to be that we could identify and complain about misguided or corrupt individuals in high places; now it is hard to see the man for the role behavior, or for the "image" of him that has been fabricated. Instead of good or bad decisions by responsible officials, we now have mediocre decisions by anonymous committees. When vast networks of functions somehow lead to immoral effects, we can find no individual to blame, no one who feels personally responsible for what happened.

To the extent that adults seem to act less as individuals

than as role players, the youth is left with a sense of impotence. Contemplating vast and complex social processes, a student may ask poignantly, "What can one person do?" Education must give him insight into how our system works, and how it poses threats to individual freedom; it must somehow, despite the overpowering social pressures on individuals, give him, or help him to maintain, a sense of himself.

Any consideration of what the world will be like in the years just ahead will, of course, have to confront the problems of the Cold War, an unpopular "hot" war, and the danger of nuclear destruction. What some have called our stability in the face of these tensions might better be described as a rigidity based on the fear that if we move, something may snap. But people cannot tolerate for long such a state of tension. Wishing for genuine stability, they find it easy to pretend that everything is fine and will stay that way. Students, at any rate, tend to see present arrangements in our society as likely to persist indefinitely, provided we are not all exterminated, which for many seems easier to imagine than social change.

Of all the effects of the Cold War, the most serious has been a moral deterioration in our national life. As Thomas Mann observed, the worst thing about totalitarianism is that its opponents are led to imitate its methods. Strident voices have been demanding that we ought to fight fire with fire, and it seems to be more or less official policy that any means are justified as long as they are believed to contribute to the defeat of communism. In its political strategy our government has sought to control the press, to manufacture opinion, to manipulate people in the interests of some temporary strategy, and to bring about the acceptance of brutality as a necessary—even an ordinary—part of life. Almost any national plan for reducing the international tensions is labeled "soft on communism," and almost any plan for improving our national life has been damned as "socialistic." In short, the country has been brought to a state in which thinking itself has been impaired. When some thoughts cannot be allowed, all thinking tends to deteriorate in quality; myths and stereotypes flourish, and wishful or fearful ruminations take the place of realistic attacks on problems.

If we hope to counter these authoritarian tendencies in

our national life, if we look toward the day when apathy is replaced by a widespread sense of social responsibility, we must teach students to ask hard questions, to discuss them without fear, and to move beyond ideas that are no longer relevant.

This education for prospective citizens must look beyond narrow, nationalistic patriotism. In a shrinking world there is no place for tribalism, and the person who regards himself as categorically different from people of other national, ethnic, or social groups is living in the past and is a threat to civic and world peace. We must seek to develop in the student the capacity to look upon other people—all other kinds of people—and feel that he shares with them a common humanity. The individual who cannot do this is, fundamentally, one who cannot admit into his consciousness some of his own dispositions. Whatever he cannot recognize in himself is likely to be attributed to some "outsiders," who are then regarded with suspicion and hostility. To become a true citizen of the world, an individual must be at home with himself and able to include within his conscious scheme of things his deeper emotional dispositions. Education can, and must, help students to achieve this integration of personality.

Education for world citizenship may seem to be far removed from the more conventional business of the college, such as teaching subject matter and developing intellectual skills. In practice, however, what hinders human relations can also hinder learning. On a recent visit to a Southern college, I was told that its students were, on the whole, very bright but afraid to think—afraid that thought about certain problems would lead to alienation from their culture. And being afraid to think about some things, they were for all practical purposes afraid to think about almost anything.

This state of affairs is not limited to Southern schools. I have encountered the same phenomenon in seniors at other places —for example, at a distinguished Western university. Probably all our leading colleges contain some young men and women with a very clear conception of life as it will be for them after they have graduated; this future life, they are quite certain, will be theirs only if they do not upset the apple-cart by thinking too long or too critically about the world around them. One can almost see the wheels turning as these students ask themselves: Should they or should they not allow themselves to be influenced by this teacher or by these ideas? They act as if they knew that giving in on one point, or opening themselves to the influence of one teacher, would threaten the whole structure of beliefs and values by which they live—and want to go on living. These students are nonthinkers, and to free them of their fear-born parochialism is one of our great educational tasks.

Today's college student needs preparation for a world in which he must play a variety of roles and even adopt new roles, perhaps several times during his life; an impersonal world in which he must nonetheless manage to remain an individual and assert his individuality; a world with an awesome potential for either utopia or disaster. How can the college possibly teach this student all that he must know?

The answer is, of course, that it cannot. What the college teaches and how well are far more important, I believe, than how much it teaches—explosions in knowledge notwithstanding. It is time for us to act on the knowledge that education is not a matter of how much content has been poured into the student and that educational growth is not a one-to-one correspondence with lectures attended. Dramatic changes can begin in a moment, under the right circumstances, regardless of the amount of material covered. Most often these circumstances will involve a personal encounter between the student and an admired faculty member. Educational history may well be made by the first college that reduces the amount of material offered in its curriculum in order to give the faculty time to reach the students. The time has come for us to control our zeal for imparting knowledge and skills, and to concentrate our efforts on developing the individual student. This is not a new idea in education, certainly not to liberal educators, but in recent years it has too frequently been neglected in favor of professional training, which makes products of the college acceptable to the graduate schools and to industry. The colleges themselves must take the lead in showing that the well-developed individual is, in the long run, the really promising candidate.

This truth was brought home to me during World War II. In choosing candidates for OSS assignments, which were often arduous and dangerous missions, we first tried to select men who displayed special attributes—for example, the ability to suppress normal fear. Eventually, however, this procedure had to be given up. Experience showed that the special attributes often did not come through in practice, and that the persons selected were called on to do such a diversity of things and to take so many unanticipated roles that our only recourse was to look for "a good man."

By education for individual development, I mean a program consciously undertaken to promote an identity based on such qualities as flexibility, creativity, openness to experience, and responsibility. Although these qualities depend in part on early experiences, college can develop them further and in new ways, as shown by our research at Vassar College a few years ago and by subsequent studies at other institutions. Many freshmen, however, do not really expect to change much in college. One day, when I had presented some Vassar data in one of my classes, a student came to me after class and asked, "Do you really mean that I can change after all these years—that I'm not stuck with the personality I've got right now?" For him and for many of the others, this idea that they might yet develop was totally new. Suddenly convinced of the possibility of change and, more than that, of the power to change in directions of their own choice, they began reading voraciously in order to find the best directions in which to develop.

Part of this development is of course intellectual and cognitive. Beyond the specific "subject matter," we can help students to acquire such general skills as the ability to analyze and to synthesize, to handle data, to see relationships and infer meanings, to judge evidence, and to generalize—skills essential to a variety of work roles and life roles. In fact, I would like to see them taught more broadly, even to people whose work requirements are not going to be very difficult. Intellect, however, must be considered as part of the personality, which by definition includes everything that an individual has learned. Facts and principles pertaining to the "real" world of natural science and practical affairs are retained by a student to the extent that they become integral with his purposes. The cultural heritage transmitted through humanistic studies becomes a major source of symbols and images that the individual uses in expressing emotional needs and resolving inner conflicts—through imagination, vicarious living, and participation in collective myths and fantasies. This is a major difference between an educated person and an uneducated one. The delinquent boy, to take a dramatic example, is one who simply has no intellectual resources that would permit him to deal with his problems in his imagination. Physical activity and sensation are the only modes available to him for satisfying his needs.

If general education consists of what remains after the content of courses is forgotten, teachers should use whatever material they believe will best develop such qualities in their students as analytical power, imagination and sensitivity to feelings. Entering students, impatient to take their places in the world of work, often undervalue a general curriculum—especially when, as in community colleges, many students already have jobs and arrive with a strong orientation toward vocational improvement. These students will need help to understand that education is as much a preparation for the enjoyment of life as a vocational apprenticeship, and that what they do in the world of work can lead to wider intellectual interests. From retail selling, for example, one might move on to sociology or psychology.

Intellectual subjects, in turn, can be used to illuminate such practical issues as sexual morality, vocational choice, and social cooperation. It is curious how unprepared for life the graduates of our colleges are. For example, nearly half of the senior women we have studied still believe in a double standard of sexual morality—a sign that education has failed to connect with the real problems of students today. Similarly, Beardslee and O'Dowd (1962) found that students were choosing their occupations on the basis of imagined life styles, not on the basis of what work the occupation demands—a subject they knew little about. In the sphere of social cooperation, students are capable of similar naïveté. Seeking a revision of parietal rules, students at a well-known Eastern college formed a committee but were unable to function, because individuals refused to accept the majority decisions. They wanted total freedom, which to them meant the absence of any rules whatsoever.

The college that would educate students for the world of tomorrow might profitably consider how it could educate them now for the Peace Corps, how to develop such qualities as a stable personal identity, social responsibility, the ability to learn to improvise. People who have trained or worked with Peace Corps members, and who have seen the returnees, report that the best volunteers do not necessarily come from prestigeful places, but often from small colleges which few people have heard of. But they all had visions of great change occurring in their lives, and visions of greatness in the whole endeavor. Naturally, each had to have some particular competency, but once a volunteer got on the job it was not his specialty that mattered; it was his readiness to do things that nobody had dreamed of, his resourcefulness in a novel situation.

Of the thousands of Peace Corps volunteers who return each year, a large majority enter or return to institutions of higher learning. As a sort of pressure group, they are demanding that education be related more closely to the real problems of life they have met in the field. I hope they succeed, for these problems call for organized knowledge no less than our students need an education in touch with the world that awaits them.

2

Excellence for What?

The mother of a friend of mine was one of those indomitable New England characters. She was an exacting, but nonetheless sweet and serene housewife who darned socks with beautiful cross-stitches, kept her house in apple-pie order, and took an interest in her husband's affairs and in the things of the mind. When she learned that Lord Bryce was going to lecture at a nearby university, she made a great effort to go to hear him. She was dismayed—my friend said "crushed"—when the great man announced as his title, "Anything that is worth doing is worth doing badly."

This excellent lady was undoubtedly brought up to believe in the maxim "If a thing is worth doing, it is worth doing well." Such a maxim is hard to quarrel with, especially if we take it to mean that once we have decided to undertake a task, we ought by all means to do the best we can. I prefer to be a little more flexible, however, and say "to do the best we can, provided we do not take too much time away from more important matters."

I suspect that Lord Bryce was not only kidding us about America's puritanism but also drawing attention to the problem of priorities—a problem widely ignored in education during the recent celebration of excellence. This celebration has left me with two major complaints. The first is with the conception of excellence that is too vague and general: excellence without reference to any particular action or quality, or simply excellence in all things. When the word is breathed, or shouted, we feel excited or guilty or anxious—the more so because we are not clear about what we are supposed to do. The accent on excellence without definition not only cuts off the search for genuine purposes but often serves as a screen behind which people conceal their real values and intentions. My other complaint is about a conception of excellence that is too narrow. Predominant in our schools and colleges today, this conception of academic and vocational excellence is endangering some of our highest values.

Support for excellence in the abstract finds its philosophic base in American pluralism. According to this view, it is neither wise nor necessary to make any final choices among our conflicting value systems. Let people have the kinds of schools they want; let each institution be excellent in its own way. The defender of pluralism, however, remains under an obligation to make clear the particular goals that *he* is pursuing—an obligation seldom met by the supporters of excellence in general. When people in the 1930s said, "Hitler is sincere," we realized that such logic would justify anything. And when Berkeley professors in the loyalty-oath controversy told themselves, "At least we'll stick together," we found that unity is useless without clarity of values.

When excellence in the abstract is urged by persons in positions of authority or leadership, it sounds like an injunction to do more thoroughly what is already being done. Most people, I suspect, gather from all the talk about excellence that they should strive harder to be successful. Most universities and colleges conclude that they must do more of what they are doing—as soon as they can raise the money.

The question of priorities is rarely discussed in the academic world, and "excellence" is used as a slogan to justify what is often mere imitation—programs that are "new" in name only, a senseless proliferation of courses, and research projects remarkable mainly for their "soundness of method"—a criterion attainable by any mediocre scientist. Projects are chosen mainly on the basis of what others are doing, what is fashionable, and what brings in money. This striving for excellence of reputation is to be observed also in the foundations and government agencies that support research. These great public institutions look first to see what is being done at leading universities where, in turn, projects are fashioned with an eye on what the foundations "go for." While serving on the boards of several fund-granting agencies, I was distressed as much by the conservatism of our group decisions as by the timidity of the applications.

In education, the slogan of excellence is used in support of egalitarian values: not everybody can go to the university or to the "good" colleges, but there are said to be other kinds of institutions of "higher" education which do different kinds of things that are valuable in their own way and with respect to which it is possible to be excellent. The trouble with this appealing argument is that the nature and values of the different kinds of education are not spelled out, with the result that excellence tends to be defined in practice as that which is rewarded in terms of prestige, power, and money.

Accordingly, colleges that really are different are rarely imitated—no matter how great their intrinsic excellence. Antioch, with its work-study program, and St. John's, with its seminars and required four-year curriculum, are radically different from the typical liberal-arts college and even from each other; each has a well-worked-out educational philosophy, each stands high according to the criteria used by accreditation agencies, and each has been a going concern for a long time; yet the ideas that guide these institutions have not caught on in American higher education. Institutions of less than the first rank that have opportunities to change themselves look for guidance not to our variety of unusual institutions but to a few well-known universities.

Recently I visited a middle-sized public university that had been asked by the state to double its enrollment. It leaders had seen in this a chance for innovation and had asked the faculty to plan for the future, not omitting their visions of greatness. It seemed to me appropriate to speak of some of the educational failings of universities such as Berkeley and Stanford and to suggest how they might be overcome. It turned out that it was precisely these two institutions that most of the faculty wanted their university to be like. We cannot complain about the desire of colleges and universities to go up in the world. This is the American way; and we can expect that state colleges will continue to become state universities. But as long as the slogan of excellence is tied to a single model, our less prestigeful institutions will suffer the vices of that model more easily than they can approximate its virtues.

Into the vacuum created by over-accent on excellence in the abstract, the individual student and his parents are likely to put a narrow conception of "success." The "different kind" of education that is to be sought by our less talented young people is thus education for excellence in their chosen trades. No one doubts that from a practical point of view it is far better to have a trade than to have none, but this hardly qualifies as a philosophy of education for people of less than average ability. Perhaps young people learning trades are expected to go about their work in the same spirit as our New England lady. This would be a fine thing, for the excellence of this lady's work was an expression of her character, which pervaded all aspects of her life; but if it is character education that we really want, we shall have to adopt educational procedures very different from those in current use. Or perhaps people with trades are expected to find in their work the same kind of satisfaction as does the professional. In an age of automation, however, the prospects for this do not seem very good. This brings us back to the goals of education set forth in Chapter 1. The great mass of our young people need above all an education that prepares them for life outside the sphere of their occuations. To say this is not to suggest any lowering of standards of work; it is to speak of an area of activity to which the narrow conception of academic excellence does not apply.

In families where there is an expectation that the children will enter four-year colleges, academic success seems often to be regarded as the road to all that is good in life, the only measure of individual worth. Young people are under enormous pressure to do what is necessary "to get into a good college." Once there, they confront demands that have grown out of the college's concern with its own narrowly defined academic excellence. The amount of assigned reading exceeds what anyone could do intelligently, and the consequences of failure are made to appear so dire that one can hardly imagine the prospect without becoming unnerved. In a highly reputable university, investigators in the Student Health Service recently interviewed the fifty top freshmen. Few of these students had ever had a date or reported satisfaction from relations with their peers, and some were suicidal. Within one general student population, some are overwhelmed by their first sense of failure and either drop out of college or lower their level of aspiration farther than is reasonable or necessary. Others rebel and attack the system with more enthusiasm than wisdom. Many "play it cool," submitting to the pressures enough to assure themselves a reasonably comfortable place in the world, while keeping their reservations to themselves.

I am particularly concerned about these pressures because, as a teacher, I am caught up in them myself. Like other teachers, I assign about twice as much reading as I did a few years ago. The students, of course, manage this reading in the most superficial way possible; they read with the examination in view, allowing themselves no opportunity to explore the pathways, to play with new ideas, to enjoy the pleasures of an intellectual life. If an instructor were to assign less reading than average, or permit himself to toy with ideas at the expense of presenting "the facts," the students would conclude that what he has to offer must not be important and that they were not getting their money's worth. We have helped to create in students a kind of slave mentality. They relieve their guilt by doing exactly what the hard masters require; and they express hostility by doing no more, by keeping their distance, and by making sure that they remain untouched in any important way.

This is pretty grim, and it is hard to say where it will end. If one makes an effort to change the system, he is suspected of trying to lower standards. If he suggests that students have problems, he is accused of coddling them and told soundly that excellence of course requires sacrifice. I do not know whether this is an expression of the unhappiness of faculty members or whether it is due merely to our general participation in a belief system that has not been adequately questioned. In any case, we are not proceeding in a way that will give us excellence in performance, either on the job or in life. Students trained in such a system become competent technicians, but it is difficult to imagine their becoming leaders of society or highly developed individuals.

There is, to be sure, growing discontent with the narrow focus upon academic excellence as expressed in high grades and high scores on ability tests. Some authorities are protesting. They say that to avoid the homogeneity due to selecting one kind of student, we must now accent various other kinds of excellence. More students should be selected who are exceptional in art, in drama, in music, and so on. This is all to the good, but the accent is still on excellence of performance, or upon the kind of thing that will eventually lead to highly visible success in the world.

The kind of excellence that matters most for the college student today is excellence as a person. We must go back to considering the kind of person we want to see develop and the means by which we are to achieve this objective. If the compulsion to cover material were replaced by a model of human development, we could measure education less by the sacrifice it requires than by the growth it produces. Theoretical psychologists and practical educators would probably agree that complexity and wholeness are the marks of the highly developed man. By complexity we mean that his personality has developed a great number of different parts, each having its own specialized functions; and by wholeness, that his many parts are in close communication with one another, and can, without losing their distinctness, work together to serve larger purposes.

The highly developed person leads a rich emotional life. His impulses are differentiated, and he knows a variety of socially acceptable ways to satisfy them. His conscience has become enlightened, and he is no longer the slave of childhood patterns. He can judge events in the world around him realistically and respond to them appropriately, yet he seldom loses contact with those feelings deep within him which free his imagination and give meaning to his life. He is open to new experience and capable of further learning.

If excellence in the person is the full development of his human potential, how are we to judge excellence in the college? This may be done in two quite different ways. Of these ways, the

more common is to ignore the complexity of what actually occurs
during the years at college and to look instead only at the quality of
the graduating class. The other way, however, would compare the
level of development of entering freshmen with that of graduating
seniors. By measuring change rather than absolute levels, this second
way would reveal how much the college has done, as distinct from
whom it was able to recruit.

Some colleges are still in the throes of deciding which of
these goals to pursue. There is, for example, a small college in the
West that has a favorable location, a good faculty, enough money,
and good buildings. The college is now asking itself very seriously
whether to go the usual way, to make itself known as a national
institution, or whether to try instead to do its best for the local
students who now enroll there. A similar issue confronts some large
state universities, who now are asking whether they can continue to
obtain more and more government money and become national research organizations without neglecting the real educational needs
of the people in their own states.

I am afraid that most colleges in America—and certainly most graduate schools—are worried more about whom they
turn out than about how much they have done for him. They want
to upgrade themselves in the academic world and expect to do so
by recruiting "brighter" students. Then they can raise standards,
attract a better-known faculty, and gradually acquire more academic
glamour. They are somewhat like the psychotherapist who undertakes to maintain a good reputation for himself by taking only
patients who are curable, relatively untroublesome, and affluent. He
leaves the difficult, unpromising, or impecunious patients to the
beginners.

There is of course a certain logic to the policy of these
colleges and universities. If they are concerned primarily with the
quality of their products, one safe course is to start with students
who are already like the graduates they want to turn out. Many
psychologists would appear to believe that college really has no
effect, or else a uniform effect, on personality, and that any differential changes that are found empirically must be due to the "natural"
course of human development. For example, wherever we reported

on the Mellon Foundation studies at Vassar (Sanford, 1956) and described the changes in various factors of personality which took place in students during the four years of college, the first question raised was always, "Did you also give these tests to people who did not go to college? Did you measure how much *they* changed in four years?" With due recognition to the importance of adequate controls in educational research, we felt that we did not need to be overwhelmed by this line of criticism. Subsequent studies of Vassar graduates and students at other institutions have shown convincingly that the college does indeed have an influence (*e.g.,* Freedman, 1962; Heist *et al.,* 1961; Webster, Freedman, and Heist, 1962; Astin, 1963; Heath, 1965; Nichols, 1965; Skager, Holland, and Braskamp, 1966). We know that in different colleges, of quite different kinds, different degrees of change in personality occur—and these in fairly predictable ways. This means, of course, fairly uniform gains for most students, and very different changes, or no change at all, for others.

Instead of judging a college's success by who goes there and how well they are expected to do, I want to suggest that we focus on what happens at the college, on what kinds of change it induces. For example, if a college admits students with relatively primitive tastes, shallow interests, values unmodified since childhood, and rigid patterns of thinking, and if after four years it turns out students who are flexible, imaginative, discriminating and capable of self-expression, the college is undoubtedly a success. It would be a success even if none of its teachers were ever heard of outside its own locality and the level of accomplishment of its students at the time of graduation were not as high as that found in better-known institutions.

In order to plan an educational program for encouraging change, we must know more about the entering student and about the factors in the college environment that can influence him. Then we must have a theory which relates all these factors. Once the program is set up, we must be able to measure various changes in individual students. Tests should be given at entrance and again at graduation, with due attention to the controls necessary to demonstrate that observed developmental changes were actually due, at least in part, to the program. Constructing such tests is difficult; but it has already been done, for example, by Paul Dressel and Lewis Mayhew (1954) and by our group at Vassar. Using these tests, we found that students changed—those who changed at all—in certain predictable ways. On the average, students were less stereotyped in their thinking as seniors than as freshmen, less conformist, less prejudiced, more open to experience, possessed of more firmly internalized values, more sophisticated and enlightened in their views of the world, and more capable of expressing their deeper feelings. Of these changes many were due largely to the processes of the college itself.

If tests of the kind we have already used were given at a wide variety of colleges, we might be in for some surprises. It is quite possible that more desirable changes are being induced by colleges seldom heard from on the national scene than by some very prominent ones. The measurement of change offers a fair test of what a small college or a new college can do. And measures of change, when they have been adequately developed, can supply the basis for a different but highly professional approach in higher education. The educator who adopts this approach, instead of boasting about how many bright students his college can attract, will talk about how many challenging educational problems confront the college and about what he and his colleagues are doing to solve them. He will let the college be known by the change it induces.

3

Neglected Forms of Excellence

"Excellence" as a slogan may allow us to forget the object of our celebration. After being stimulated by the slogan, we must spell out what it is we want to do and, as our object grows clearer, find ways to nurture and award these specific forms of excellence.

In the promotion of excellence, punishment is generally less effective than encouragement, a fact that has led to the elaborate systems of rewards used widely in schools and colleges—*e.g.*, a prize for the best paper in a given field in a given year or an award for a distinguished career. This system of rewards may not inspire us to work harder, but it makes life in the academic disciplines more interesting. It offers an opportunity to become involved, to speculate on who will receive which reward and later to argue about the choices of the selection committees. More important, it gives one a sense of belonging to the discipline and a continuing appreciation of its values and goals. It also serves as a reminder that science is a human enterprise and that its advances are brought about by persons behaving in fallible ways.

The fundamental question is *what to reward*. One can tell a great deal about a society by knowing what kinds of heroes it has, what kinds of activities are openly admired and rewarded. I would suppose that selection committees, by and large, reflect major trends in the society. Functioning as members of the society in making their selections, they reward what is regarded as good on the basis of the underlying objectives of the society. The question is whether a body with the means to make awards can take a position *outside* of the society and make awards in accordance with the way society *ought* to go. Can it survey newer social needs and arrange to meet them? From this point of view, we would pay most attention to whatever is being neglected by the natural or automatic processes of society at a given time. For example, at present we do not have to worry about recognition for achievements in natural science. Our society has definitely been won over to this field, and we can be sure that people who achieve in it will find their just rewards. Similarly, given the current mood of the country, we do not have to worry lest insufficient attention be given to the identification and encouragement of bright youngsters. Meanwhile, other potentially fertile fields, now rather neglected, could be made fruitful through the provision of rewards.

The Dissensual Disciplines. Fields such as engineering and animal husbandry are useful, unthreatening, and thus approved by nearly everyone. As Frank Pinner (1962) has pointed out, however, other disciplines—such as the social sciences, poetry, and art— are "dissensual" in the sense of arousing public anxiety and mistrust. Other things being equal, a body that sets out deliberately to make awards should give first attention to the dissensual areas, assuming that the consensual ones will take care of themselves.

The Builders of Bridges. In our age of specialization, most awards are given for achievements in narrow fields. A man without a specialty has no place to go. For example, I know a man whose interests span physics, art, and psychology. When he visits American universities, he is as likely to fraternize in one of these departments as in another. He is responsible for an invention which has virtually transformed modern life, and he is capable of coming up again with something equally startling. But this man cannot find a job in an American university because he is not sufficiently identified with or "trained" in one of our traditional disciplines.

Again, the department of speech at one large university includes people trained in such diverse fields as philosophy, law, sociology, English, psychology, anthropology, and history. The department is not a very happy one. It has been described as an aggregation of displaced persons. They carry on scholarly work, but much of it—because it bridges two or more fields—goes largely unrewarded. In a fresh consideration of awards, should we not assume that each discipline will take care of its own and turn our attention to activities that extend beyond the existing disciplines? Instead of giving prizes for history, for example, we might reward the best piece of psychological work by a historian or the best piece of historical work by a psychologist.

Such rewards are all too rarely thought of today. In fact, instead of building bridges among the disciplines and showing students that knowledge, like the developed mind, has some fundamental unity, many college teachers are contemptuous of any efforts in this direction. One of the favorite clichés from the colleges is that an interdisciplinary course is a watered-down course, that the only way to keep up standards is to insist on close involvement with the specialties. Teachers in general education curricula sooner or later come to be regarded as second-class citizens by their colleagues in the specialized disciplines. If we wish to counter this trend, we should encourage the search for knowledge based on a synthesis of developments in two or more existing disciplines.

The liberal-arts colleges still speak as if they sought to develop a man whose knowledge is, in some sense, general and all of a piece. Who in our society represents this ideal? Such a man would no doubt be hard to find, but if he could be found he should be rewarded. It is hard to know how else the image of the generally educated man can be socially sustained. We cannot maintain the liberal tradition merely by preserving the liberal curriculum in our colleges and telling our students that everything correlates. Somebody has to represent this tradition in his life.

The Excellent Teacher. Despite all the talk about the crucial role of the teacher in our society, and despite all the stress on "good teaching" by the colleges, we have found virtually no ways to reward excellence in teaching. As a matter of fact, teaching at the college level can hardly be called a profession. Though the Ph.D. is said to be a college teacher's union card, the degree requires an apprenticeship not in teaching but mainly in research methods. Nor is the newly hired instructor taught how to teach—an omission that results partly from the paucity of general theory about teaching, partly from the lack of procedures by which the new teacher can be helped to improve his work. He is seldom observed at his work, except by his students, and among college teachers the subject of teaching is nearly taboo. In these circumstances it is useless to talk about rewards for good teaching. Such rewards cannot be based on reports by students or on gossip collected by the president; they should probably be based on the judgment of peers.

Excellence Not Measured by Grades. Whereas the aims of liberal education are stated in terms of individual development, success in education is still almost always measured in terms of grades—which, according to many teachers, often express their estimate of the student's developmental status in a clumsy, partial, and misleading way. Webster, Freedman, and Heist (1962) have listed the known inadequacies of grades as measures of educational achievement. In a study at Vassar College, Donald Brown (1962) asked faculty members to nominate students as "ideal products of the college." He found that teachers could agree quite well as to who these ideal products were, but the association between being nominated and receiving top grades was not very close. Among the students receiving the highest grade-point average, only about half were nominated. These students made a far better showing in the psychologists' estimates of their stage of development and potential for future development than did the high-achieving students who were not nominated. In giving awards to students, we must learn to supplement grades with more flexible and sophisticated measures.

Group Efforts. In addition to many types of individual awards, I would advocate that more attention be given to rewarding groups. James Coleman (1959) found in the high schools he studied that talented youngsters devoted their greatest efforts to athletics— the only activity which served group goals and enjoyed group approbation. In our society, intellectual and scholarly work tends almost always to be individual and competitive, at least during the earlier training stages. We have rarely found ways to put the *social* needs of young people into the service of worthy scholarly or cultural endeavor. School work is usually regarded as a fairly grim and self-centered business, based on the principle of every man for himself. It is sharply separated from social life, which is carried forward in the peer culture and frowned upon by faculty.

Coleman argues persuasively that a group effort can produce intellectual work of high quality. Mature researchers sometimes derive enormous satisfaction from collaborations, though of course they may have some headaches from it, too. Today, young people seem to be naturally group-oriented and given to cooperative enterprises, especially if they feel that they, as opposed to their elders, are running things. Can we not help them to organize their social needs in the interests of intellectual and cultural aims? If we could create situations in which an individual is rewarded for intellectual achievement by the group of peers whose good opinion he values most highly, he might learn relatively early in life that such achievement does indeed have a social purpose. At some colleges, for example, the interfraternity council recognizes the house with the highest scholastic average.

In order to encourage excellence, however, we must do more than reward it after it happens. We must nurture and channel it from early childhood. Common sense suggests that, in this nurturance, we should train specific skills rather than develop the whole personality; but research has shown that creativity, for example, is not a learnable skill and yet it is more than a native talent that blossoms by itself. Instead, it is a disposition of personality, which develops through parent-child relationships, the educational process, and the adult work environment—a disposition that draws on personal discipline, a reservoir of conflict-free energy, a sense of social responsibility, and the capacity to work harmoniously with others.

The pursuit of excellence requires a recognition that the human individual is all of a piece, and that his diverse features develop in interaction one with another. Conceptually, we can separate intelligence, feeling, emotion, and action; but none of them functions independently of the others. Just as development of the whole person depends heavily upon exercise of cognitive functions, the cognitive normally develops in pace with the rest of the personality. Without humane feeling, intellect can be monstrous, and feeling without intelligence is childish or dangerous.

In spite of this interdependence, educators are widely charmed by the idea of a disembodied intellect whose sole fucntion is the intake, storage, and reproduction of data. I am afraid they derived this curious idea not from the observation of what goes on when students learn in college, but from reading psychological literature. Psychologists have abstracted processes such as cognition and learning from their living context, seeking to isolate them experimentally in the hope of obtaining precise information with which to demonstrate general laws. In consequence, there is a vast literature—and even a vast, indigestible undergraduate curriculum—in which perception is treated independently of the perceiver and learning independently of the learner. Ironically, these vaunted general laws derived from laboratory experiments are not really general at all, for they break down as soon as a new variable is introduced. In the classroom, for example, numerous additional variables are at work, so that only very rarely can the findings of the learning laboratory be applied directly to the school. But we should not blame the present generation of psychological experimenters too much. They were usually taught by college professors who thought they could train the intellect without touching the rest of the personality. These professors were under the influence of the know-nothing behaviorism of the 1920s, itself an outgrowth of a long tradition in which the narrowly cognitive or mentalistic dominated Western approaches to knowledge.

Beyond the teaching of facts and the training of skills, excellence requires development as a person—the sort of development that liberal education can assist. According to research by MacKinnon (1961) and his colleagues at the Institute for Personality Assessment and Research at Berkeley (Barron, 1963; Crutchfield, 1963; Gough, 1960; Helson, 1961), the most creative people in architecture, literature, mathematics, and engineering science are distinguished from less creative ones by, among other traits, their greater flexibility of thinking, breadth of interests, autonomy, and integrity. In college, these same traits are more typical of seniors than of freshmen—the result of an intervening expansion and differentiation of the personality.

Education must provide for the different paces at which such development proceeds, and for the many forms it may take. In the current effort to reconcile the fact of large individual differences (in talents, interests, and motives) with the need to help each student to develop as a person, many schools have chosen to segregate the gifted children. Although this arrangement simplifies the teacher's job by narrowing the "range of talent" to which he must respond, the practice of labeling certain students "gifted"—and, by implication, labeling others "not gifted"—is of dubious value. Often the "accelerated" child simply learns more material at the expense of other kinds of personal development; and often a child placed in a slower class is simply a "slow starter" who would ordinarily be destined to achieve great things, but only after early academic struggles. This practice makes no allowance for the truly able child who is prevented by cultural or psychological handicaps from performing well in school, although recent research (*e.g.*, McClelland *et al.*, 1958) shows that these so-called noncognitive factors can turn a child with high ability into a low achiever.

Although performance in high school is correlated with scores on ability tests given in elementary school, and performance in college with grades in high school, the correlations are not very high. Among the many exceptions to the common trend, I am particularly interested in youngsters who quickly reach a high level of intellectual activity and then, as if burnt out, develop no further. I am even more interested in those who have undistinguished records in school and even in college, but find themselves later on. For example, I know a woman who failed to graduate with her class in a British public school and who was regarded as the dull member of the family. Her father kept her in the same school because he could think of nothing else to do with her. Three years later she passed the university entrance examinations at the top, and went on to become a distinguished biologist and psychoanalyst. Similarly, a physician who became director of a great foundation and profoundly influenced medical and psychological research in this country once told me that he was forty years old before he began to feel he might possibly amount to something. Through school, through college, and through medical school he had compared himself unfavorably with a "gifted" friend and classmate to whom everything "came easy," but a comparison of their careers after forty clearly shows the superiority of the late maturer.

At the University of California's Institute of Human Development, researchers currently are examining people, now thirty-five and forty years old, who were studied intensively during their early years (Macfarlane, 1960). The unexpected is almost the rule. In numerous cases, extremely unpromising youngsters somehow found themselves later on—even as late as thirty or thirty-five; and in other cases, the stars of elementary and high school classes achieved very little later in life or even became clear failures.

In spite of these considerations, colleges are even more preoccupied than the schools are with the cognitive aspects of development. The symptoms are overspecialization, overemphasis on grade-point averages, and the slogan of "raising standards"—often a euphemism for increasing the burden of meaningless assignments. The picture is not so bleak as this suggests, however; for in comparison with the mood that prevailed on campuses during the 1950s, college educators today are showing more real concern for the student as a person. They are beginning to apply what amounts to a new psychology of the curriculum, of teaching, of teacher-student relationships, and of student peer cultures; and in doing so they are asking broader questions about how diverse parts of the college environment actually favor or hamper student development.

Even when an individual has achieved a high level of personal development, and hence an ample disposition to excellence, he may not be able to do excellent work—or at least not creatively excellent work—unless conditions are favorable to it. The needs of the creative worker are seldom understood. Even university departments, schools, laboratories, or institutes do not always provide favorable environments for creative work. There are colleges, for example, in which a creative man's style and habits of work might easily cause him to be labeled a deviant, with the result that he would receive little encouragement for what he wanted to do.

Although competition may stunt some forms of creativity, life in the departments of leading universities today is likely to be highly competitive. In contrast, departments before World War II were usually still human communities in which different professors had different roles and functions: as critic, teacher, benevolent supervisor of graduate students, writer of papers and books, innovator, and so forth. In these settings individuals could express themselves, and the two or three truly creative people (all that it took to make a department famous) could rely upon colleagues for various kinds of support. Today all department members are expected to be stars, or to have built into them before they arrive or before they are promoted, everything needed to be productive. What the recent pattern lacks is a style of relaxed symbiosis that often led to highly creative work. Today's high-pressure departments are affecting not only scholars but the creative people in literature and the arts drawn to academic positions by the rather obvious financial and social advantages over life in the garret. Solitary work can sometimes be harrowing, but we can only wonder how much freedom the writer or artist surrenders in exchange for the new "security." In any event, it makes little sense for institutions to recruit creative talent without providing a setting in which it can flourish.

Finally, one of the most important elements for the environment of excellence—the one most often lacking—is the presence of at least one person who really values imaginative and useful work. If this person is in an administrative or supervisory position, so much the better. Probably in our efforts to stimulate greater excellence at all levels, our first priority should go to developing leadership. Above all, we need key people who have themselves achieved a degree of excellence as persons, so that they can appreciate and encourage it in others.

4

The Students
We Teach
Today

If one works in academic institutions over a long period of time, he is impressed not so much by the differences among generations of students as by the similarities. In watching filmed interviews with some of the Berkeley students who took part in the 1964 revolt, I was struck by how much they resembled the young people of my own day and those whom I knew at Vassar during the 1950s. No doubt there is something new in the current attempt by students to reform the educational system and to have a greater voice in determining their own education; but the behavior of those at Berkeley was not uncharacteristic of college students of any period. And the adults involved also behaved true to form.

All generations of college students have in common their youth and their developmental status. Typically they have problems of identity and self-esteem. They are idealistic and easily disillusioned, especially when the adult figures they admire seem to have feet of clay. They are torn between loyalty to old values and to others newly found. They demand independence, but need assurance that adult authority stands firm. At the same time, most undergraduates are still free of the responsibilities and commitments that people assume as they enter adulthood. This is why a student can join a march in Mississippi one year and decide in the next to become a corporation lawyer.

In view of this special freedom, adults in our society sometimes depend upon the youth to initiate social change. They are counted upon to do the kinds of things that adults, because of their commitments, are in no position to undertake. This may also explain our mixed feelings toward them; for on the one side we tend to live vicariously in them, to identify ourselves with some of their radical or offbeat doings, but at the same time they make us nervous because we are not entirely sure they are going to settle down in a few years and be just like everybody else (though, of course, they nearly always do this). I can recall the disappointment with which a group of businessmen greeted the news that college students on the whole are basically conservative. These men had supposed that all college students were like the activist minority, and that this was how it was supposed to be—radical when young and conservative thereafter.

In a rapidly changing society such as ours, we should expect that people brought up in one period will naturally differ in some ways from people brought up in another period. Students are affected, often in a deep and lasting way, by the climate of opinion that prevails during their college years. In the research at Vassar College (Sanford, 1956; Freedman, 1962), we studied various generations of alumnae: the class of 1904 to the class of 1954. In the attitudes and values of each group, we could see a reflection of the climate that prevailed when that group was in college.

A college climate is determined in part by the faculty, who, like the Vassar alumnae, bring to the present many values from their own college years. Our senior faculty of today, for example, was influenced strongly by the Depression, which denied to some the leisure for a liberal education and led many to set a high value upon economic security. With this background, they were in no position to resist a trend toward specialization in education or to devote themselves primarily to the university's more liberal values.

Among student generations, we know most about those of the 1950s. Various researchers found the students of that period to be passive, conformist, uninterested in politics, focused on their own private interests, fond of comfort, and eager for a secure place in society. In young women this syndrome was marked by a flight into femininity and, among the Vassar girls we studied, by a desire to have about four children as quickly as possible: a woman's place was in the home, where she would meet her warrior at the door with a bowl of hot wine as he came home from work.

These attitudes were influenced not only by a faculty withdrawal into the areas of their professional concerns but by the state of our society during the 1950s. During that period there was a relative shortage of young people of college age, which had resulted from the lower birth rate of the Depression years. At the same time, there was great emphasis on economic growth and national security. Such a combination produces conservative ideology. We find in the educational thinking of the 1950s a heavy accent on science, special programs for the gifted, high standards and increasing toughness in education, and a gradual speeding up of everything. Education was geared to produce young people who would strengthen the society and its economy.

Colleges took advantage of this situation to upgrade themselves. As the government began pouring money into higher education, especially at the graduate level, in order to speed the training of people who were needed in the increasingly complex machinery of society, professors took advantage of the new generosity to further their own specialties. In the late 1940s, for example, we in the psychology department at Berkeley saw our chance. With grants from the Veterans Administration and from the U. S. Public Health Service, we introduced new programs of graduate training and embarked on larger, more specialized research projects. We worked to advance our science, and it did not occur to us that the other departments were doing the same thing and that the result would be a serious neglect of undergraduate education.

Undergraduate students, however, did not object. They could see that by doing what their teachers said, by taking full advantage of the new opportunities for training, they would move into society faster and find places that would be suitably rewarding. In this context, the mid-1950s White House Conference on Education had a hollow sound. Educators spoke of the great aims of liberal education, but their actions revealed a primary interest in preparing young people professionally and vocationally.

Within the past decade, however, social needs have shifted. No one is complaining about the shortage of young people, for we seem to have an endless supply. The economy, bolstered anyway by automation, puts less pressure on young people to jump into jobs merely to keep the machinery going. Meanwhile, more than a few students have been inspired by the Peace Corps and the civil-rights movement to pursue larger goals than getting good grades, being admitted into a good graduate school, and having a good job.

In contrast, most colleges are still reacting to the needs and fashions of the 1950s—still engaging in a sort of assignments race, which may improve their standing among academic institutions but which cannot improve education.

Another source of student unrest is the new meaning of the old conception that colleges stand *in loco parentis*. Originally the conception implied not only discipline but generous, personal help. As colleges have grown and "raised their standards," however, the nurturing functions of the college have been eroded or neglected while the control and punishment functions have been maintained. This in itself creates a revolutionary climate. In family life, the child who is ignored except when it is necessary to punish him may soon be on the road to becoming a rebel or delinquent. Students for many years surrendered their rights as citizens in exchange for the special care and attention that parents or college were expected to offer. Now, with the care and nurturance gone, students not inappropriately demand their rights. This is not because students are less in need of what colleges might do to develop them; it is because they find themselves in a situation that is essentially unfair and would induce rebellious feelings in people of any age.

The dissatisfaction of undergraduates is echoed today, as it seldom was in the past, by the graduate students. Before the recent, drastic expansion of graduate programs, students could feel that upon admission to a department, they were joining the community of scholars. Today, however, they suffer increasingly from the same kinds of pressures and constraints, the same burden of meaningless work, as do undergraduates or even high school students. As departments have grown larger and more professionalized, traditional communities of scholars, embodying graduate students and professors with whom they worked closely, have been disappearing. The graduate student is being confronted with a series of hurdles that involve even more serious consequences than do undergraduate tests and is under pressure every minute of his day to think and act within the confines of his profession's requirements. He must, in effect, surrender himself to his profession. He cannot investigate what he is curious about but only what can be investigated by approved methods. He has little time to explore other fields or even to get beyond a specialized area of his own field, because whoever is in charge of his work often demands more than can reasonably be done. He cannot ask questions of a sort that might broaden his mind because he cannot afford to display any ignorance. He cannot converse in the language of educated men because this might be interpreted as professional impurity.

Graduate students are cynical about this system. They say that they will stay with it only until they get their "union card"; then they will be free to inquire as they please. But even before they receive their degrees, they begin to be aware that the constraints will be nearly as great after they have actually entered the profession. Acceptance of graduate school requirements brings about an identification with the system that is very difficult to shake off later.

Graduate students also have many occasions to lament their wasted years as undergraduates. They specialized in those years, thinking that in graduate school they would find freedom. Now, when they look back from their new vantage point, they see that they lost the best opportunity to pursue their genuine interests and explore new ones when they were undergraduates. Hence they have a natural inclination to relive their own undergraduate years vicariously through the students who are now entering college. Or if they had a good undergraduate experience, they feel sympathy for their younger brothers in the large universities.

In sum, graduate students have been changing sides, as many did at Berkeley in the fall of 1964. Finding the channels into "management" too narrow, the effort to negotiate them too costly in other values, the rewards of belonging to the governing body too remote or otherwise dubious, they have been casting their lot with the "workers." As leaders of student movements, they have the advantage of longer experience at the university; and as future teachers, they have a greater stake in reform than undergraduates, who could decide to put up with a bad situation until summer or graduation.

Another mark of today's undergraduates, as compared with those of ten years ago, is their greater sophistication. This is a credit to improved education in the high schools. It seems also to be a result of greater mobility and experience of the world. Many students have studied or traveled abroad, been in the Peace Corps, or had extraordinary experiences in social action. Professors who have been shielded by the lecture system may not realize how critical some students have become, how impatient with perfunctory teaching and textbook generalizations. No longer willing to take things on faith, they want to know the sources of information, and even how the data were collected. When a representative of the State Department spoke at Stanford, at a "teach in" on the war in Vietnam, he cited a precise number of North Vietnamese said to be fighting in the South. The students laughed at him. What aroused their scorn was not the claim of infiltration but the pretense that our government knew exactly how many had crossed the border.

In the new situation that has developed, we may anticipate educational innovation and reform. Changes will be guided by increased understanding of students' needs, but it may take overt protests to set them in motion. Experimentation has been promoted by educators on many campuses during the past ten years but not much happened until after the 1964 revolt at Berkeley. In 1963, Professor Joseph Tussman of that university first proposed his experimental college, a two-year program on the model provided originally by Meiklejohn at Wisconsin, but action was delayed until student protest had aroused fears and guilt within the faculty.

In the years immediately ahead, there will be less accent on educating students to man our system and more on educating them to participate in its benefits. Prominent among these benefits is an opportunity for a broader education—an education which helps us to enjoy a world beyond our jobs, as well as to adapt resourcefully to new roles produced by technological and social change.

Students are sternly challenged by the world as it now is, and to face the changes we know will occur, they need a triple preparation. As future jobholders, they must be taught how to grow in their work and to meet demands now unthought of; as citizens, to help direct the uses of technology which might otherwise go its own way; and as men, to discover through the arts and humanities a perspective broader than the demands of work or even the immediate society. Since 1965—known by some as "The Year of the Student"—educators have seemed increasingly willing to meet this triple challenge. A colleague has told me that at the Danforth Conference on Higher Education professors and deans turned away from previous arguments that an interest in student needs would transform the college into a kind of psychiatric community. Instead, they showed a growing concern with students as individuals—their developmental status, their feelings, their purposes—and with detailed planning of educational improvements. For a long time now I have been arguing that we should encourage students to criticize the education we arrange for them, and that we should consider their suggestions thoughtfully. In the light of our sudden upsurge of sympathy with students, however, perhaps I should add a reminder that they also need reassurance that the institution is in the hands of authoritative adults. At colleges such as Antioch, where students are given all the rope they can use, officials soon discover how conservative students are when allowed to govern themselves. Innovation is encouraged neither by a denial of adult leadership nor by an effort to keep the students "in their place," but only by a willingness to listen to them and then to do what their actions show they need.

II

Personality
Theory

5

Styles
of
Authority

Since students are affected not only by what the teacher says but by the way he treats the class, psychologists have taken an interest in measuring the developmental effects of various teaching styles. In an autocratic style, for example, the teacher imposes goals, gives orders without reasons, and relies on threats. In contrast, the teacher who assumes what Harold Anderson (1939) calls a "socially integrative" style relies less on blame than on praise, admits his own doubts and even errors, and seeks the child's acceptance of the school's goals. By developing a way to measure these two styles, Anderson found that the former leads to resistance or overconformity by the child, and the latter to a growth of initiative and spontaneity.

In experiments with eleven-year-old boys at the University of Iowa, Ronald Lippitt and Ralph White (1943) showed how groups respond to each of three different "climates"—authoritarian, democratic, and *laissez faire*. In an authoritarian climate, such as Anderson's "autocratic" teacher might produce in the classroom, the group becomes either "aggressive, irritable, self-centered" or else "submissive, highly dependent, socially apathetic."

When the reaction to authority is submissive, the group works harder than it would in either the democratic or *laissez faire* atmospheres, but when the leader leaves the room, their zeal leaves with him. In the *laissez faire* situation, where the leader plays a minor role, the group loafs or plays randomly—a sign that its members need and want some kind of direction. Between these two extremes, the democratic atmosphere promotes "group morale" most successfully: by offering guidance but avoiding autocracy, the leader teaches his group to work together for common goals and to continue their work even when he is temporarily absent.

Although Lippitt and White were cautious or perhaps modest about carrying their conclusions into the realm of educational and political philosophy, other writers (*e.g.,* Erikson, 1955) have not hesitated to suggest, for example, that the political organization typical of Nazism was made possible by the kind of authoritarian child training traditional in Germany. The Iowa studies also led G. Watson (1940) to declare that "there is only one way in which democracy is to be saved . . . the adoption of day-by-day methods of democratic work." While sympathizing with such a statement, one wonders whether teachers, particularly teachers of young children, do not find such exhortations confusing or even exasperating. From some of the discussions of democratic methods they could easily get the impression that if children are just allowed to do what they want, everything will be fine; and that if teachers try to exercise their proper authority, the charge of "dictator" may be hurled at them.

In view of this confusion, we ought to reexamine the distinction between *autocracy* and *dominance,* keeping in mind the developmental status of the child and the ultimate aim of his education—a mature and informed personality. In doing so, we should ask, for example, whether a firm, authoritative teacher might not only have the smoothest-running classroom, even in his absence, but also be most loved by the children. Furthermore, since authority can vary not only in degree but also in style, and instead of discussing how "strict" a teacher should be, we might achieve more by distinguishing clearly between the styles of autocracy and of dominance. In the former style, a teacher would determine what a child does regardless of his wishes. In the latter, however, he would work to integrate the child's aims with those of the school—a form of dominance that I believe is often necessary, compatible with the democratic spirit, and seldom harmful.

Whenever we make a child do something that he does not want to do or prevent him from doing what he wants, we are exercising dominance—whether we use threats, forceful orders, persuasion, or subtle play upon his feelings. I doubt that anyone ever raised a normal child or saw a class through a school year without employing some of this flexible control. In this sense, we exercise dominance not only in the service of cultural ends but also in the name of nothing more than the teacher's or parent's convenience; for if the child is to appreciate our respect for his individuality, he must learn to respect that of others—even adults.

Autocracy is something else. It is defined not so much by the frequency with which a teacher performs specific acts (giving orders, for example) as by the general quality of all or most of his acts: by the way he sticks to his policy regardless of individual differences among children, of variations in the same child's psychological state, or of the requirements of a particular situation. With the slogan that discipline must be complete or there is no use having any at all, he treats a minor breach of the rules no less severely than a major infraction.

What causes autocratic behavior? Seldom is the answer clear to either the teacher or the students forced to obey his commands and prohibitions. From dynamic psychology, however, we learn that such behavior often occurs when a teacher (or parent) has to communicate to others a set of standards he never really accepted but against which he is afraid to rebel; when he seriously doubts his ability to cope with children in a group and is plagued by visions of chaos; when he is filled with anxiety because the children display (or seem about to display) reprehensible tendencies that he still finds difficult to control in himself; or when, out of temporary frustration or continuing unhappiness, he just wants to punish somebody. In these circumstances, the children become as anxious as their rulers; and if they fail to rebel, it is only because they are afraid to.

Hardly less harmful than autocracy is its well-intended opposite—the failure to adjust a permissive and democratic philosophy to the developmental status of the child. In order to grow into our culture, a child *needs* authority to help him establish control of basic emotional impulses. To the extent that a child is left without adult control, he must rely upon his own inadequate devices; and when his untutored impulses arise, he is thus at the mercy of imaginary punishing agencies, which grow in frightfulness as the impulses increase in strength. When he is allowed to do just as he pleases, to impose beyond reason on the playful or tolerant or inhibited adult, his anxiety about punishment increases until he practically begs—by increasingly naughty behavior—for an adult to step in. His need for authority is unlikely to be met or even understood, however, by a teacher or parent who fears being disliked if he is firm, who is so full of inhibited aggression that he fears one forceful act would give him away completely, who out of persisting adolescent rebellion is determined to reverse all the practices employed by his parents, or who with the best intentions is trying to achieve a misguided style of "liberal" behavior. His children will continue to suffer anxiety, and may later depend on external authority to supply the stability they never had.

With increasing age the child's capacity for self-control, his ego, increases. He not only needs less and less external control but may become increasingly resentful of it. At this stage, we should pay increasing attention to the child's wishes, not because they are more important than our own but because we need to strengthen his ego through exercise of it, through allowing him to participate as fully as possible in decisions concerning him. Throughout this delicate transition, we should keep in mind that a child is harmed by premature liberalism as well as by autocracy, for both discourage self-control—the one by placing too heavy a burden upon it, and the other by allowing no exercise of it at all.

Presumably the teacher wants the children in his care to be happy and spontaneous *now* and also to develop into effective democratic citizens. The adoption of day-by-day methods of democratic work may teach a student to work with others, assuming the methods are suitable to his age; however, he will learn how to think for himself only when he has developed a genuinely internalized conscience. Without it, the student remains weak in the face of demands from external authorities such as the gang, the narrowly defined social group, or those who claim to represent the will of the people or of God.

Parents are more important than teachers in establishing conscience in the child. As the ego develops and the normal process of identification with parents goes on, these external authorities become increasingly a part of himself. This development takes place most smoothly when suitable firmness is accompanied by ample love. The teacher cannot be a crucial influence one way or the other in this matter, but he can do much to reinforce the normal process, and can refrain from disrupting the delicate structures being developed.

What the teacher does to promote harmony and co-operation in the classroom also favors the normal process of character development. But it is well also to consider that spontaneity, initiative and ease in social contacts with peers do not necessarily hold the most promise for future development. Indeed, it may be the other way around. A child in whom the process of internalizing parental values is taking place may well be inhibited, shy, sensitive, or overly dutiful.

As a child develops, he needs an image of authority he can accept and make his own—authority employed in the service of cultural values, with respect and love for the child; but as he adopts these values, the external pressures can gradually be relaxed. At each stage, teachers and parents should offer as much democracy as the growing ego can handle, and as much dominance as necessary for the transfer of cultural elements and for the reduction of anxiety about punishment.

6

Development
through
Challenge

In planning for the needs of
students, we must keep in mind
a theory of how they ought to develop. There is no shortage of
goals: in sketching the ideal
graduate, educators speak of
maturity, of effectiveness, of
creativity, of "positive mental
health," of stability. As the list
grows into an incantation, we
are tempted simply to nod our
approval and maybe add a goal
of our own. To clarify the theory
of development, however, we
need to ask how these goals
differ and what each one offers
and omits.

Take maturity, for
example. In a statistical sense,
the word might refer to those
qualities more typical of people
over twenty-one than under.
Within a given population, such
qualities could in theory be
measured and a typical portrait
drawn, but this portrait might
leave out such "childlike" qualities as wholeheartedness or spontaneity. According to this definition, maturity would call for no
special effort by educators or
their students, but only for a sort
of cultural conformity. In using
maturity as an educational goal,
therefore, we must take care to
employ a definition based not on
what the common man is but on
what our students, with help,
could become. In this normative

sense, maturity refers to the extraordinary adult—the man who not only deals effectively with the world but also leads a rich impulse life and continues to enjoy the imagination lost by so many in childhood.

Like the term maturity, "positive mental health" can be taken in two ways. As outlined by such writers as Marie Jahoda (1958), it offers a complex and admirable goal, including such criteria as sense of identity, grasp of reality, and potential for further growth. In lesser hands, however, "positive mental health" can shrink to no more than a synonym for stability—a single quality among the many we need to consider.

For a goal more inclusive than stability and less ambiguous than maturity, we can turn instead to personal development—not a quality to attain, but a process to live. Long before we "reach maturity," this process includes a succession of stages, and in each we are called upon not only to learn the appropriate routines but also to face the unsettling strains which lead us in time to the next stage. "Stability" in leading the life of a given stage—of adolescence, for example—is seldom admired for more than a few years. What we do admire is competence in dealing with the world one knows, coupled with a curiosity about the unfamiliar and an ability to find in the psychic household a place for whatever curiosity brings home.

One of the oldest and deepest issues in psychology is that of persistence versus change in personality structure. Although all theorists conceive of personality as a more or less stable structure, some accent the "more" and some the "less"; some are inclined to stress the apparent fixity of inner structures and the continuity of the past and the present, while others stress change with circumstances and the possibility of new beginnings.

In common sense and in folklore the two views seem to compete on more or less even terms. Faced with the persistent misbehavior of a child, some of us say, "It's a phase, he'll get over it"; others foresee a delinquent career. A friend tells us that as a result of his marriage he is a "changed man," but all we can see is the charming ne'er-do-well that we have known for years. His wife, a converted environmentalist, believes that if he has not changed, he will, for she has a grip on some of the major determinants of his behavior. A student at the beginning of his sophomore year tells us that he has seen the light, that he is going to quit wasting his time and conducting himself in such a way as to merely get by. Most of us, perhaps, recall that we have heard this before and respond with extreme skepticism, but one of the student's advisors assures us that he really has changed and deserves to be encouraged. Some college seniors say they hate to think of what they were like as freshmen; others—not knowing, perhaps, that they were supposed to change— can think of no ways in which they differ from their freshman selves; still others report many ways in which they have changed but are more impressed by their sense of continuity with their past.

Selection procedures, which undertake to predict future performances, assume the persistence of abilities; but people outside of professional psychology resist the idea that an individual's fate should be determined by psychological tests administered at the age of eleven or at seventeen—tests of doubtful validity but so impersonally crushing to those who do badly as to become a self-fulfilling prophecy, and so compelling a model to those who succeed as to confirm them in a narrowly cognitive pattern of education.

In the psychological literature, persistence and change are accented in widely varying degrees. Among the advocates of fixity, some stress genetic or constitutional factors, while others are more impressed by the impact of the environment during the early years of the individual's life, such as the childhood traumata and repression emphasized in classical psychoanalysis. In contrast, situationism, field theory, and phenomenology accent the possibilities of change, through responsiveness to new situations or through the bringing to bear of cognitive abilities that have been developed.

Exponents of early determination and fixity have in the past not so much denied the possibilities of later change as merely neglected to study them. In recent years, however, some psychoanalysts and other dynamic psychologists (*e.g.,* Erikson, 1955; Keniston, 1965; Sanford, 1966; White, 1952) have taken an interest in the phenomena of late adolescence and young adulthood and produced some new concepts to account for change in these age ranges. (They do not, of course, believe that changes at this time are discontinuous with the individual's past.) At the same time, exponents of late determination and changeability have been hard put to demonstrate the kinds of changes which their theory would lead them to expect. Research on college students, for example, has shown that although some of them develop in accordance with hopes and expectations, others go all the way through college with the same motives, the same attitudes and values, the same outlook on the world with which they began. Faced with this evidence, virtually all personality theorists today recognize the necessity for dealing with both persistence and change, for distinguishing among environmental conditions, kinds of structures in the person, and resulting kinds of changes.

Although the terms change, growth and development are sometimes used interchangeably, it is useful to distinguish among these three processes. As the most general term, *change* embraces both growth and development, and other phenomena as well. It may be desirable or undesirable, progressive or regressive; it may involve diminution as well as increase, decline as well as development. In the study of personality, it is useful to distinguish between changes in the amounts of variables and changes in the relations among variables. For example, college seniors may have less achievement drive than freshmen, but such achievement drive as the seniors do have may be organized with greater attention to real possibilities.

Growth may be defined simply as expansion of the personality—the addition of parts (*e.g.*, habits, needs, or beliefs) and the enlargement of existing parts (*e.g.*, an increase in the intensity of a need). If we conceive of personality as a system, we may regard its growth in the same way that we regard the growth of any other system (a city, a university, or a department of the university). Growth may or may not be "healthy," in the sense of being favorable to the over-all functioning of a system; it may indeed be malignant. How favorably or unfavorably we view the matter depends heavily upon the degree to which growth is accompanied by development.

Development means, most essentially, the organization of increasing complexity. For example, a child behaves in an all-or-nothing fashion because his personality is very much all of one piece.

With time, various sub-systems become differentiated and take on particular functions; and without losing their particular identity, these sub-systems become integrated into larger wholes in order to serve the larger purposes of the organism.

In children and young people, psychological growth and development are clearly associated with increases in chronological age, only in a general way: each individual proceeds at his own rate, and sudden upswings in the growth or development of some particular features may be followed by periods during which nothing seems to happen. In adults and older people growth and development may, and often do, occur, but their association with chronological age becomes highly tenuous.

In studying changes in personality, the psychologist is confronted first by the question of how his subject differs from the last time he was studied and then by the question of what the differences were probably caused by. For example, he may ask how a group of sophomores differ from what they were last year or the year before that (longitudinal study). On the other hand, he may ask how this group of sophomores differs from a group of freshmen (cross-sectional or panel study). Sometimes the psychologist may focus on a single variable, such as independence of thinking: Does individual A show more or less of it than he did before? What of this group of individuals who are being studied longitudinally? What is the average amount of independence found in freshmen, in sophomores, in a national sample of eighteen-year-olds? How much variation is there around the mean for the educational or age group?

Answers to these questions are often of considerable practical importance, since actions affecting groups have to be based on conceptions of group norms; but what we most want to know, to continue with the present example, is what determines independence of thinking. Knowledge that a variable such as independence of thinking increases with age, within certain limits, is an aid to explanation because it narrows the field of inquiry, focusing attention upon certain age-linked factors. We must, however, go on to ask why the variable increases with age. What events occurring at particular times actually induce the observed change? What stimuli could be introduced at the present time to increase independence of thinking?

We study causation with reference not only to a person's current psychological system but also to his peculiar history. In the first kind of study, people are subjected to the same stimulus situation to see how they will respond, and their average response is said to exemplify the operation of a general law. In virtually all such experiments, however, there are individual differences—variations around the average response. To the stimulus situation, people bring different readiness for response, presumably because they have been subjected in the past to different influences. These individual differences call for historical study of the unfulfilled needs and unresolved conflicts which began in the subject's past and are now organizing much of his behavior. In addition, understanding of the present sometimes requires attention to the future as well as to the past, for unfinished business of the personality may include not only the working out of past dilemmas but the promotion of long-range objectives. To appreciate these objectives, and to understand how behavior is organized in their service, it may be necessary to extend "the present" in which a subject is studied, following him a way in order to make sure of the direction that he is taking.

How does a person change through interaction with his environment? In response to this fundamental question, each school of psychology offers a theory. We cannot do justice to them all here and must be guided mainly by what has been called the prevailing functionalist point of view, which states that a person strives to reduce the tension caused by a challenge and thus to restore equilibrium. The child comes into the world with natural susceptibilities to tension; internal or external stimuli immediately arrive to make tension actual (to arouse, in other words, a drive or need) and thus to induce striving. Unless the child's need is immediately taken care of by other people, the striving will continue until he has found some means for reducing tension and restoring equilibrium. With repetition of the stimuli and of successful striving, the child soon shows an inclination to seek the objects and to utilize the patterns of action that served him. He has now *grown,* for the personality contains a "need-image-of-object" and a "need-pattern-of-action" that it did not contain before. The child would no doubt be content to go on using his new-found patterns, but it soon turns out that they are not adequate to new stimuli and tension states, and thus the whole chain of events begins again.

The state of equilibrium to which the individual attains after striving is not the same state that existed before the tension-inducing stimulus arrived. After each successful striving, the organism is slightly changed; and since a diversity of needs must be taken care of, change is rapid during the early phases of the organism's life. This means that the equilibrium that is attained has to take into account the organism's increased size and complexity. It follows from this formulation that an expanding personality not only fails to regain its earlier stable states but also opens itself to new kinds of tension. The objects and activities that come to be included within the personality structure, because of their role in reducing tension, themselves begin to lay claim to some of the available energy. At the same time, the growing personality becomes the object of an increasingly variegated set of demands from the external environment. With more needs there is a greater possibility not only for frustration and conflict but also for growth. Thus, the goals of "adjustment," "stability," and "peace of mind"—if these terms refer to a general state of freedom from tension—are fundamentally incompatible with the goal of development.

It is the expansion of the personality that makes development necessary. Just as a business corporation cannot exceed a certain size without breaking into smaller sections and developing a more complex structure of control and administration, so a personality cannot expand beyond certain limits without increasing in complexity. Different functions have to be assigned to different parts; channels of communication among the parts have to be set up, and diverse activities have to be coordinated or brought together in larger units.

This way of looking at growth and development is most often encountered in discussions of what happens in childhood, but I would argue that the same general principles hold for the adolescent years, and afterward. Of course, it is commonly assumed that a high school or college student will not learn unless he is motivated, and a great many different needs that might be served by the student's diligent performance of his academic work have been noted: curiosity, interest, self-esteem, vocational ambition, desire to please parents or leaders, and so on. But I am concerned not so much with what induces effort as with the conditions and processes of change in the structure of personality. The essential point is that a person develops through being challenged: for change to occur, there must be internal or external stimuli which upset his existing equilibrium, which cause instability that existing modes of adaptation do not suffice to correct, and which thus require the person to make new responses and so to expand his personality. If the stimuli are minor or routine, the child, instead of changing, will simply react as he has before.

It is because of their greater repertory of routine responses that students and adults do not change as readily as children. The dynamics of change, however, are essentially the same in all three groups, and if appropriate stimuli are applied, students and adults *will* change. We need not wait for them to "grow naturally" under conditions of comfort or protection (we would wait a long time, according to the present formulation); nor should we suppose that once people have become "mature," no more developmental change is possible.

It follows from this same formulation that "resistance to change" does not require a special explanation; it is in the nature of the phenomenon we are studying. For example, a student entering college has a wide array of adaptive mechanisms and ways of ordering experience—mechanisms that have served him well in the past and are serving now to maintain his stability. If he is eager for new experiences, as he often is, what he anticipates is not so much change in himself as the successful testing of powers he already has. When confronted with challenging situations, he first calls into play his well-tried responses; and when this structure is finally replaced, his natural inclination is to make the new structure do for all future contingencies. It is the job of the educator to keep challenging this structure in the interest of growth—a job made difficult by the "prematurity" of many college students, who feel they already know what they want to be and how they want to live.

Unfortunately for educators, this problem of premature certainty is complicated by another. When a child is confronted with crises that are too much for his adaptive capacities, he falls back upon primitive defensive stratagems. The same thing may happen to the college student: if we propose to challenge the student and so to upset his equilibrium, we must, of course, draw a line at strain that would be so great as to cause defensive reactions to be switched in. The danger in college, however, is much less than in childhood with its peculiar combination of frustrations, conflict, and threats. In thinking about child development, many have concluded that all we need to do is protect the child from these sources of tension—a view applied indiscriminately to college students more by parents and some psychiatrists than by educators. In contrast, the theory of this chapter is that people develop when stress is great enough to challenge their prior modes of adaptation, but not so great as to induce defensive reactions.

How much stress does each student need? In college today one observes some young people whose environments up to this point seem not to have offered enough in the way of challenge: everything has been so well planned and executed by knowledgeable and kindly parents who could afford the best, that the student has had little occasion to extend himself. He gives the impression of a simple, secure, good-natured, and naïve person who is neither troubled nor troublesome. It is not that growth and development have been rendered impossible or extraordinarily difficult, but rather that crucial stimulation has yet to occur. On the other hand, the great majority of entering college students bring with them the after-effects of earlier struggles with overwhelming tension, and it is probably safe to assume that none is absolutely free of unconscious motives and mechanisms of defense.

Changes over time in children and young people usually have a progressive character: the individual remains in a "stage" or "phase" for a time before passing on to another, which is marked by greater expansion and complexity of personality and bears some kind of dynamic relationship to the processes of the prior stage. Among the conceptions of stages of psychological development that have been offered, the most influential have been those of Freud (1917) and of Erikson (1955). Freud differentiated stages of psychosexual development according to the order in which the several erogenous zones of the body become focal in the production and release of tension. Erikson has proposed eight stages of ego development, each of which is defined mainly in terms of the kind of attainment that makes it possible for the individual to move on to higher levels of development: basic trust, autonomy, initiative, industry, identity, intimacy, generativity, and finally, ego integrity.

Two basic conceptions are necessary to the explanation of observed sequential changes in personality. One is the idea of *readiness*, the notion that certain kinds of responses can be made only after certain states or conditions have been built up in the person; and the other is that change in the personality is induced largely by stimuli arising either from the person's bodily functioning or from his social and cultural environment, and that the order of events in the personality is largely determined by the order in which these stimuli are brought to bear.

The idea of readiness underlies many of our common-sense practices in child training and education. We suppose that a particular kind of experience, such as going to school, studying arithmetic, or going away from home for a time, will have beneficial effects because the child or young person is ready for it; and if some ordinarily salutary set of events, such as going abroad or getting married, proves to be disappointing we are quick to think that the individual was not ready for it. But just what conditions in the personality are favorable to a particular kind of developmental change when a particular kind of stimulus is brought to bear? Erikson's formulation of stages of ego development is a system of hypotheses bearing on this point. The attainment that is characteristic of each stage is regarded as a condition necessary to progress toward a later or higher stage. For example, a young person can establish a suitable ego identity only after he has achieved an adequate measure of independence from his parents; and he can lose himself in a relationship of genuine intimacy only after his identity has been stabilized.

Although a condition of readiness is necessary to further development, it is not a sufficient cause of such development: the personality does not just unfold automatically according to a plan of nature. Whatever the stage of readiness in the personality, further development will not occur until stimuli arrive to upset the existing equilibrium and require fresh adaptation. What the state of readiness means, most essentially, is that the individual is now open to new kinds of stimuli and prepared to deal with them in an adaptive way.

In the case of children and young people, many such stimuli make their appearance in a certain order and are often of sufficient potency to have a determining effect upon the order of events in the development of personality. At the same time, each culture has some kind of general plan in accordance with which individuals are introduced to many of the major experiences of life. There are times when it is considered appropriate to go outside the home to play with other children, to go to school, to go away from home, to go to work, and so on. Within a group of children adequately prepared for a given challenge, the typical behavior that results may be ascribed in large part to the culture pattern.

Individual differences in *rates of development* are a striking phenomenon in our society. In a group of people of the same age, we may often observe individuals who are taken up with problems which are typically confronted at earlier or later ages. Among college seniors, for example, the majority are concerned primarily with finding a place within the larger society, with vocational and marriage plans; but many will have settled these questions earlier and will have been marking time, while many others will still be struggling to gain control over impulses, to overcome their dependence upon their parents, to achieve accuracy in their perceptions of reality or even to establish basic trust. The present view of developmental sequences seems to offer an approach to the explanation of such individual differences, based upon the wide variations in readiness of the personality and in the timing of stimuli from outside. If with Erikson we conceive of a succession of attainments each of which is necessary to later developments, we have to deal with the possibility that the individual might be delayed or "fixated" at any one of these stages. What often happens is that the stimulus situation, the "crisis" in Erikson's sense, which might have led to adaptation on a higher developmental level was actually too much for the individual and evoked, instead, a defensive reaction involving unconscious mechanisms—a reaction which prevents an adaptive resolution of the crisis.

At the same time, in our highly diversified society, with its socioeconomic classes and religious and ethnic groups, there may be wide variations in the quality and timing of challenging experiences, even though most people accept the same general plan. Events such as weaning, being given responsibility for other children, the first heterosexual experience, and getting a job may occur at different ages and in circumstances that give them different degrees of potency. As suggested earlier, some college freshmen seem relatively underdeveloped because of their protected lives and lack of experience. On the other hand, it often seems that what lower-class children gain from variety and intensity of experience in certain areas is more than counterbalanced by a history of events that could not be properly assimilated or that led to maladaptive reactions.

The question of what is the optimum rate of development is a highly complicated one for which no satisfactory answer has as yet been found. Our culture in general favors as the ideal a long period in which the child and the youth are encouraged to develop before adult responsibilities are taken up. It is commonly assumed that, within vaguely defined limits, the longer this period of preparation, the richer and more productive the adult life will be. The value that we place upon four years of college is based in considerable part on the assumption that the readiness for future experience that is built up during the college years will make all future events more meaningful and increase ability to meet them in ways that expand and develop the personality. We have as yet little solid information about this. It is not difficult to find college graduates who support the assumption just stated. But one may also find individuals who failed or wasted their time in college, or did not attend,

but who "found themselves" later on and attained extraordinarily
high levels of development. According to the theoretical position
being developed here, we should emphasize the distinction between
arrests of development due to unconscious defensive reactions and
failures to develop because of lack of challenge. With respect to the
former, the college may postpone specialized intervention as long as
the conscious ego is continuing to expand; but with respect to the
latter problem, it should not just wait in the hope that a young
person will naturally develop "from inside." Surely we can afford
to be deliberate about introducing young people to the major challenges of adult life, but there would be no advantage in this unless
the time thus gained were actually filled with experiences that develop the personality.

7

Self-Knowledge

A college is not a therapeutic community, but its educational procedures must be guided in part by knowledge of how the unconscious influences other processes, such as learning, and how it may be modified through education. Learning is blocked wherever unconscious processes prevent the individual from having the necessary experience, or where defensive mechanisms come so readily to the fore that new adaptive responses have no chance to be tried. These barriers to learning are readily to be observed among college students— in the girl who fails at economics because she cannot seriously entertain any ideas that might threaten her special relationship with her father; in the boy who cannot work because he fears that any achievement by him would give away his desire to get the better of his father; in the large number of students so taken up with problems of sexual morality, or sexual accomplishment, that they have little time for anything else.

It is no wonder that some psychiatrists, familiar with unconscious processes and their enormous implications for the student's future, have considered that the most important step in the development of the entering student is making these processes conscious, thus permitting the ordinary educational procedures to do their work. While no one suggests that all or even most students should have psychotherapy, it has been cogently argued by Lawrence Kubie (1954) that educators must find some way to lead students toward that "self-knowledge in depth" which is sometimes attained in the consulting room. One can only agree with Kubie's general aim: the college offers an opportunity to reduce the number of graduates who now enter mental institutions or who begin psychotherapy after having caused all manner of psychological damage to other people, and educators ought not to be satisfied with a system that permits its graduates to put skills and knowledge into the service of unconsciously determined and socially destructive systems of belief and attitudes.

Education cannot simply take over the techniques of the consulting room, nor does it need to. Happily for the theory being presented here, and for what seems to be the position of most educators, not all of the student's functioning is dominated by unconscious processes. Even students who show obvious "symptoms" of neurosis have large areas of their personality open to modification through experience. Knowing the potency of unconscious processes, the college teacher is completely justified in devoting himself to ordinary educational procedures, which can expand that part of the student's personality that is not dominated by the unconscious; and even the college psychiatrist undertakes not to give the student a full course in self-understanding but to work with him just long enough to remove whatever is spoiling his role as student. The assumption is that as the consciously determined parts of the personality expand and develop, the unconsciously determined parts will shrink in relative importance. As our understanding of the entering student increases, we may know how to attack the crucial problem: how to tell the difference between unconscious processes which can determine the whole course of the educational experience and will yield only to special therapeutic procedures, and those which may be expected to wither on the vine as the conscious ego expands.

We have distinguished two ways of promoting development of the personality: (a) expanding those parts of the personality that are not dominated by unconscious processes and (b) making the unconscious conscious or, in more general terms, modifying unconscious structures and changing their relations to the conscious ego. The former seems clearly enough to be represented by ordinary educational procedures that challenge the student's beliefs or require him to take new social roles. What about the latter? It will be argued here, first, that education can help to make unconscious processes conscious and, second, that education is the best general means we have for transforming unconscious impulses so that they may be not only gratified but brought into the service of conscious purposes.

In psychotherapy, unconscious motives and unconscious defenses against them are revived or "relived"; they are "transferred" to the therapeutic situation and, *while active,* are made the object of interpretation. Unconscious processes become conscious in these circumstances because unconscious motives naturally seek realization in action and because the patient's ego, which naturally seeks an adaptive synthesis of all the individual's needs, now has a potent ally in the ego of the psychotherapist. The major principle at work is, once again, that of tension reduction; just as the id lends energy to the ego because of its success in satisfying needs, so in psychotherapy older maladaptive responses will be given up as the ego with the help of the therapist learns to carry on its work more intelligently and efficiently. The tension-reduction principle may operate in another way to further the purposes of psychotherapy. Maladaptive defenses are maintained because any relaxation of them is an occasion for anxiety; but once the patient has transferred his infantile wishes and attitudes to the psychotherapist, the therapist then can arrange things so that the patient or client will experience more anxiety at the prospect of disappointing the therapist than at the prospect of allowing repressed impulses or ideas to find their way into consciousness.

The teacher as well as the psychotherapist may become an object to whom childish attitudes are transferred; and the student, in his relations with a teacher who comes to mean something to him, will call into play the same resistance to self-insight that is exhibited in psychotherapy. The crucial difference between psychotherapy and education is that a teacher uses the student's transference not as a means for giving the student insight into himself but as a source of motivation for the student's intellectual work. For example, the student may be striving to please the teacher or to be like him.

There are many other procedures commonly used in various kinds of psychotherapy, such as giving support, offering advice or direction, letting the patient or client talk about himself. A teacher might, if he chose, use any one of these procedures on some occasions. The question is whether the processes which operate in psychotherapy have their counterparts in education or in other non-clinical situations. It has been suggested that they do. For one thing, we have seen that the unconscious may become conscious in psychotherapy because of the strengthening of the ego—a process that may also occur through learning from experience in natural situations. Quite conceivably, the conscious ego may thus become strong enough so that its readiness to assimilate unconscious impulses and ideas is as great as that achieved by most patients. There is probably nothing comparable to the correct interpretation of a patient's unconscious processes at times when those processes have come to the fore, but there are various kinds of situations outside the clinic in which a person's attention is drawn to his own processes in a way that might well lead to a broadening of his consciousness—given sufficient strength in the ego. For example, a teacher of literature may insist that his students understand fictional characters before judging them. If the student's ego is unprepared, he will fail to "get it"; but if it is, his understanding of himself will increase with his understanding of others. Again, the college student is very likely to observe others—teachers and students whom he admires—doing what he unconsciously would like to do; and thus unconscious motives are stimulated to express themselves in awareness at a time when the ego is supported by the example of others.

Particularly important for self-knowledge are changes in a person's objective relations to others, such as occur when new social roles are assumed—changes that may reduce the necessity for repression even as they require cognitive reorganization. Thus, when a girl has a baby of her own, she is often able to understand her mother in a way that she never did before. She may not be able to say what has happened, nor is there any need to; the important thing is that a different role brings a different relationship and a different self-conception, so that the girl is able to see and to respond to her mother more as she really is and less on the basis of imagery acquired in childhood. Similarly, the student who does not understand his teacher now may very well do so when he becomes a teacher himself. I recall a graduate student who for the six years of our intimate association always acted toward me as if I were a particular kind of childishly conceived father. This misconception had to be endured because it favored good work by this student, and in any case it would probably have yielded to nothing short of intensive psychotherapy. But when this student moved to another university and had graduate students of his own, the misconception was soon cleared up; and in this case the formerly unconscious ideas and attitudes could be verbalized.

In sum, unconscious processes may become conscious under natural conditions in the normal course of events. It is possible for a teacher to speed up this kind of developmental change by educational means, given sufficient knowledge of personality functioning. On the other hand, in some cases ego development has been so retarded and the personality is so largely dominated by unconscious processes that special psychotherapeutic means are called for at once. How may we tell the difference between such a case and that of a student who, despite the display of some symptoms, is able to go on developing under the impact of education? At the present time this is a diagnostic point of considerable subtlety, to be simplified only when we know more about both personality and about the process of education. It seems safe to say, however, that a college ought to be able to tolerate a large amount of "symptomatology" in students (excepting gross signs of psychosis) as long as these students are able to enter with some enthusiasm into some part of their college work.

Modifying unconscious processes and making them a part of that synthesis which the ego seeks to achieve is not entirely a matter of bringing them into awareness or making students capable of reporting on them. Unconscious motives strive for realization in action, but they will settle for expression in fantasy or in vicarious living. Here education has a crucial role to play, starting in the

early years and continuing through college. By making available to
the individual the symbols of our culture, it may vastly expand his
capacity to find gratification in imagination rather than in compulsive action or in mere sensation.

The present theory concerning the relations of impulse
and imagination originated with Freud, who suggested that in an
infant the frustration of a need is followed immediately by an
image of something that would be gratifying. Amid infancy's many
frustrations, fantasy thus arises naturally in what Freud called "the
primary process," the source of later poetry, art, and other creative
products. The generation of images is in itself gratifying to the
child, despite the possibility of adult displeasure at "idle" fantasy.
As he grows, however, the child needs to share certain of his fantasies and to extend his range by learning what others have dreamed
of. For the latter purpose, reading is essential, and once the necessary
symbols have been acquired, books can help to gratify as well as to
refine some of our most primitive emotional needs.

All of this has implications for practice. It is sad that
many children read without enjoyment, perhaps because they have
been introduced to reading not as a means of satisfying their impulses, but as a duty. Teachers must somehow counteract this prevailing notion. Perhaps the earliest developmental task in education
is to teach every child to enjoy reading, making up stories, and doing
other imaginative work.

Cultivation of the child's emotional life can strongly
influence his much later education. In my own observations at
Vassar College, for example, it was clear that "good" students—
those who performed very well academically and showed signs of
creativity—differed from other students in what they had to say
about their play as children. The good students had more often
played alone, made up games to play, engaged in play acting, enjoyed imaginary companions, read and been read to. In other words,
for these more creative students, the life of the imagination was
allowed to be, or by some accident became, important in childhood;
they went on from there to scholarship and an interest in the things
of the mind.

According to our theory, the individual who has learned

to use his imagination is not merely in touch with his impulse life but has actually expanded it. In my view, this happens as the symbols of our culture become available to the individual, enabling him to deal with his basic impulses through fantasy and through his imaginative participation in literature as well as plays, movies, and various other art forms.

It is not difficult to teach children to enjoy imaginative work, even after their earlier and spontaneous imaginative life has been dampened by "realities" which adults present to them. I had the experience of trying to persuade ten-year-old boys to produce Thematic Apperception Test stories. At first, confronted with the task of making up a story about a picture, they denied that it could be done, but I found that if I coaxed them to say *something,* and then used what they said as a basis for more encouragement, they finally produced a story. The production in response to the next picture came a little easier. And so we proceeded into the psychological realities of their lives. I would say that almost any child can be persuaded to forget earlier prohibitions against being imaginative.

When children are beginning to read, the content ordinarily does not matter very much, provided it has interest. If comic books will induce them to read, let them read comic books. The "act" of reading at an early age can later become the "art" of reading. Collective fantasies expressed even in the most atrocious of the comic books are probably less antisocial than what any child is himself capable of thinking. There is a kind of socialization at work in the sharing of any kind of collective fantasy, however primitive it might seem.

In her book *Spinster,* Sylvia Ashton-Warner describes how she was able to teach the Maori children of New Zealand to read. They had in the beginning no conception of school, and they sat day after day, year after year, without learning anything. She found, however, that she could get at the fantasy life of these children, and then connect a few words-to-be-taught with what she knew to be a basic interest or fear. And thus a start was made.

The big problem, of course, is how we can keep the young child's imaginative life going even after he gets into the second or third grade, where he has to concentrate on learning about reality so that he can make predictions of what might happen, gain a sense of confidence in his ability to judge events, and thereby learn to make decisions about what he is going to do. Often, it seems, a child leads a wonderfully imaginative life until he is about five; and then he is taken into school to be given the discipline thought necessary to function in the modern world. The great task for the teacher is to develop the higher ego functions without obliterating the rich emotional life of the child.

With the aid of a developed imagination, the individual may expand and release his impulse life without jeopardizing his integration. By making the cultural world available to the student by teaching him the use of symbols, we enable him to perform all kinds of psychological functions that would be impossible if he were restricted to transactions with concrete things. Only in this way can adults remain civilized while gratifying the infantile needs that are still very much with them and which demand satisfaction.

III

Aspects
of Student
Development

8

Social Responsibility

One of the first reviews of *The American College* (Sanford *et al.*, 1962) appeared in a Polish newspaper. While approving of our general approach to the college as a social institution, the reviewer argued that the goal of a college education is not individual development but the improvement of society, and that the success of a particular institution can be judged only by the social contributions of its graduates. In reply to this criticism, I would say first that although we wrote mainly about personal development, we assumed, as did the Declaration of Independence, that fully developed individuals would naturally be concerned about the public welfare.

Some of the socialist countries, such as Poland and Russia, have shown that they know a great deal about how to win young people's devotion to the purposes of the state—a devotion sustained by the intense need of a relatively underdeveloped country to increase production and by the unanimity of parents, schools, and government officials in telling young people what they should do and be. Responding to the obvious need, these young people are apparently able, at least in their teens, to feel that they are giving freely of themselves. There is no evidence that their unquestioning participation in socially useful group activity necessarily impairs future development of the personality. It seems obvious that the countries concerned could not run at all if the responsible adults did nothing but conform blindly to dictates from above.

Among the questions raised by this kind of society, however, is the degree to which it depends upon ethnocentrism, upon the categorical rejection of outgroups such as the "bourgeoisie" and "aggressor nations." Socialist nations, of course, have no monopoly on nationalistic "patriotism," for this can be found in some degree in any country and is generally encouraged by governments. In college, however, we seek to develop a higher order of social responsibility, which consists of loyalty to certain ideals that the individual understands, rather than to an aggregate of people whom he regards as being like himself. Naturally, loyalty to these ideals does not preclude opposition to others, but we should base our judgments upon principles, not upon the notion that other groups are categorically different and therefore irredeemably inferior. Such notions may help to sustain social effort within a nation, but they meanwhile increase the risk of war.

In contrast to ethnocentrism, social responsibility must be developed, not merely appealed to; and during the 1950s our colleges were criticized widely for failure to develop it. In a discussion of several studies, Jacob (1957) contended that students were focused on a narrow, private sphere of interests, on how they and their families could benefit from society, but rarely on what they might do for it. In another interesting study, Gillespie and Allport (1955) compared the attitudes of our students to those of students in a dozen other countries. To an Egyptian villager, for example, an education means the opportunity to do something for his people, while to our students it meant the promise of summers on Cape Cod. To describe this lack of interest in public affairs, Riesman (1960) coined the word "privatism."

During this period, we were studying students at Vassar College (Sanford, 1956), and we did find that, compared to earlier generations, these girls were intent on getting married and leading comfortable lives. What impressed us more, however, was that during college they were changing in what we considered to be favorable ways, and that as seniors they were relatively more restless and dissatisfied than earlier in their college careers. In general, they had become not only more accepting of themselves and of other people as individuals, but also less ethnocentric, authoritarian, and conventional in their thinking. It seemed to us that the changes in such students promised well for their future, even though they were not expressing any great intentions at that time to go out and reform the world.

In writing about students during the 1950s, my inclination was not to blame them for their conformity but to point instead to the state of affairs in the nation as a whole. With the Cold War in full swing, and the nation caught up in a surly, automatic anti-communism, students were under great pressure to take their place in a society that, so they were told, had already developed as much as it was going to and that needed only a firm defense against its enemies. In those years, there was little to inspire sensitive or idealistic young people; and to the extent that students are different today, we should credit the difference mainly to changes in outlook that pervade the whole society—changes such as the civil-rights movement, the Peace Corps, and the fresh accent on social welfare.

Even today, however, the proportion of students who are involved in social action is popularly overestimated. In a longitudinal study of student development at Berkeley and Stanford, Katz (1966) concluded that "activism" had attracted only about 15 per cent of the students. In 1961, the initial interview of the Student Development Study at Stanford included an item about interest in public affairs. After about two thirds of the freshmen sample was interviewed, it was discovered that no one had indicated such an interest; so the item was dropped. Four years later, some of the same students were asked, "Which of the following experiences or activities have you engaged in during your college years?" Of the activities listed, six referred to political activity. As shown in the accompanying table, responses to these items suggest that in 1965 most of the seniors were apathetic about political issues. When these same students were asked to list the organizations and clubs that had been most important to them during their college years, very small proportions (never more than 10 per cent) listed groups for civil rights or for other political study or action.

The picture is much the same when students were asked about their future lives. The task was to "rank the following interests and activities according to the relative degree of importance you expect them to have in your life after graduation." The list of 14 items included "participation in activities directed toward national or international betterment," "participation as a citizen in the affairs of your community," and "helping other people." None of these three items was ranked in third place or higher by more than 11 per cent of the students.

Even the Free Speech Movement at Berkeley attracted only a minority of the total student population. In the fall of 1964, at the height of the controversy, Professor Somers (1965) of the Sociology Department questioned a representative sample of Berkeley students about their attitudes on the matter. He inferred that, of 27,500 students, about 30 per cent agreed with both the goals and the tactics of the "militants," another 30 per cent agreed with the goals but not the tactics, and 22 per cent agreed with neither (with the rest "undecided"). Even among students sympathetic to the cause, most usually sat on the sidelines. The largest demonstration drew about 6,000, or less than a fourth of the student population; and those who staged the Sproul Hall sit-in, presumably the most dedicated, numbered about 800. Somers points out that more than half of the militants were supported by their parents, some of whom were faculty members at nearby institutions.

Probably the 6,000 at Berkeley who demonstrated for free speech were not very different from the 5,000 who signed a petition in support of their professors during the loyalty-oath controversy in early 1950; and the "campus radicals" of the 1930s were probably about as numerous, proportionately, as the "activists" of today—just numerous enough so that colleges such as Vassar were described by local citizens as "hotbeds of radicalism."

Along with a radical minority, our colleges have long been populated mainly by students who care little for politics and who generally reflect the conservative views of their parents. I re-

Percentage of Stanford and Berkeley Men and Women
Engaging in Political and Social-Service Activities*

	"Frequently"				"Occasionally"				"Never or almost never"			
	Stanford		Berkeley		Stanford		Berkeley		Stanford		Berkeley	
	M	W	M	W	M	W	M	W	M	W	M	W
Civil-rights activities in or near school	4	7	4	5	16	20	14	19	81	73	82	73
Civil-rights activities in other states	1	1	0	0	4	3	0	1	95	94	99	97
National or community political activities	4	4	4	2	26	34	22	27	70	62	74	70
Campus political activities	8	8	7	4	23	26	21	24	69	66	78	71
Service activities off campus—work with unemployed, minorities, etc.	8	9	3	10	17	31	12	33	75	59	84	39
Student committees, etc.	15	22	7	14	38	42	23	29	47	34	70	57

* Based on responses in 1965 of approximately 500 senior Stanford men and women (about half of the graduating class) and approximately 600 senior Berkeley men and women (about one-third of the graduating class)—all of whom had earlier taken part in a survey of freshmen.

member that when we were in college, professors tried in vain to interest us in national affairs; but the events that concerned us occurred not in the larger world but mostly on campus, on the football field, or perhaps midway between us and the women's college across the lake.

In order to help students increase their sense of social responsibility, colleges need a theory of how that sense develops as children grow. A child cannot develop except through interaction with other people. In particular, he needs a family, and in time he develops attachments to them. In order to sustain these attachments, he has to carry out some obligations to the people around him. At first he is hardly to be differentiated from the group with which he lives, and he will love others in much the same way that others love him. He incorporates into his personality much of what is there in the social environment. If the social environment is loving, he tends also to be loving, and his obligations to other people become closely tied to his obligations to himself. Gross failures in social responsibility, such as marked selfishness or aggressive self-seeking, are always tied to failures or distortions in these early familial and social relationships.

As an integral part of his need to be protected and loved, a child normally desires to give something to others, to give himself to causes or to enterprises in which he joins with others; and this becomes a basis of his good conscience and his self-respect. Chiefly as an outcome of struggle with his own antisocial impulses, the young person becomes more idealistic. In order to master his impulses, he strives for a kind of perfection and sets for himself high goals of moral achievement, which are accompanied by high expectations of other people. Meanwhile, the adolescent begins to shift his attachment from the family to groups outside the home. Often adolescents like to lose themselves in a group, to be fully accepted by it, uncritically loyal to it, and indiscriminately hostile to outgroups that seem to threaten it. At this stage, ideas of right and wrong are often based on the thinking of the group or of its real leaders. The individual likes to perform hard tasks in the interest of the group, and to be rewarded by it for what he does.

This unquestioning loyalty later may be generalized to larger social groups such as the nation, in which case we find the kind of nationalistic patriotism discussed earlier. But uncritical devotion to any group is a lower order of responsibility, for it does not require much ego or personal development or even much education or intelligence. Moreover, it is likely to be impermanent. It dissolves when the group dissolves, because it constantly has to be sustained by group influence.

By going through this stage and then growing out of it, an adolescent learns not only to work with others but also to be wary of blind loyalty or the uncritical rejection of other groups. A youngster who misses this stage in high school ought to have a chance to go through it in college. I am thinking, for example, of an intellectual or aesthetic boy who never played with rough fellows, but came home instead to mother and his homework. When he arrives at college, this sort of boy usually rejects sports and other group activities, including everything that in our society has been a normal part of life among men, and goes on to become an intellectual or specialist so lacking in social feeling and techniques that he is alienated from the rest of society.

In order to avoid both alienation and the compulsion merely to "do one's duty," a person needs the experience of group loyalty followed by a chance to criticize the group and to compare it with others. In the latter stage, he will probably become disenchanted, as students often do, with his college, his community, his nation. He will complain about hypocrisy and phoniness and point readily to adults' failings. Meanwhile, his own values are challenged by exposure to other cultures and to new kinds of experience. After a few lectures on anthropology, especially on sexual customs, students often see that we have one way of doing things and others have another, and that between the two there is little to choose. "What is good for her," as the Vassar girls used to say, "might not be good for me."

Many students resolve the conflicts created by disenchantment and by their introduction to the relativity of values by returning to a traditional value orientation after they graduate from college; others discover that there are group goals and purposes that can be accepted *after* they have been critically examined, and that the pursuit of these goals may serve a number of basic and persisting needs of the personality. Ideally they may find, in socially valuable work, satisfaction for a whole range of needs—both higher needs for good conscience and for self-respect and lesser needs for mastery, achievement, self-expression, or recognition. In a fully integrated personality socially responsible behavior can be a channel through which even childish needs can be expressed. One can, if he is sufficiently developed, find in group solidarity some of the same kind of wholeness that the child enjoys; only now it is on a totally different level because it is more conscious and therefore more susceptible to control, when this is needed.

From a developmental viewpoint, the task of the college is large. Freshmen are not very far along toward development of the kind of social responsibility of which I speak. Generally, they are still caught up in problems of authority and are inclined, when the chips are down, to do what authority says rather than what they themselves have thought best. They are in a very poor position to take responsible action on the larger social front, often because they lack self-confidence and have an uncertain view of what they can do. They are also taken up with other problems.

In spite of this preoccupation with self, students at a liberal-arts college do develop in the direction of mature social responsibility. In tests such as we have done, at Vassar, Stanford, and Berkeley, this development is reflected not by a prevalence of civics-class slogans but, for example, by a decline of ethnocentrism. When students are asked to respond to an attitude scale made up of items that state what a "good citizen" ought to do or that express approval of existing institutions, seniors actually obtain lower scores than they did as freshmen.* In the Vassar research, we interpreted this change, with the help of other evidence, not as a decline in social consciousness but as a growth in nonconformity. Knowing some of these seniors, we did not believe for a moment that their increasing skepticism or even cynicism concerning family, church, and state would lead them to neglect their civic responsibilities or to be unresponsive to human needs. What we found reassuring was the fact that these increasingly independent, critical, and nonconforming young women were the same ones who showed the sharpest decline in ethnocentrism and authoritarianism. As their faith in institutions went down, their faith in themselves and in others generally went up.

Increasingly mature judgments about how society works (and ought to work) are seldom produced simply by "citizenship education." Although courses in government can awaken the critical spirit that may lead a student to his larger concerns, courses are regarded in general more as the subject of examinations than as a challenge to the way one lives. In order to strengthen social re-

---

* One of the tests we used at Vassar in the mid–1950s was the "Social Responsibility" scale of the California Psychological Inventory (Gough, 1956).

sponsibility, the college must worry not only about its curriculum but about the values it lives by, the example it sets.

To change values fundamentally, we take a student from a community such as high school and help him to become a reasonably compatible member of a new community in which different values are expressed—values we hope the student eventually will assimilate. Newcomb (1943) demonstrated this process of acculturation at Bennington College, where the faculty and older students represented a consensus of values, which new students gradually came to accept. The same point has been vividly demonstrated in St. John's College in Annapolis and at Reed College, where there are single, "monolithic," faculty-student cultures and where students who choose (and are chosen) to stay have no alternative to participating in that culture.

At a minimum, assimilation of the values of a college culture may involve little more than a shift of adolescent loyalty to a new and larger group. Often there is merely an exchange of traditional values for prevailing ones, conscience thus changing in content but not necessarily in structure nor in its connections with the rest of the personality. We noticed at Vassar that if, after sharing in the culture of the college, a graduate married a man who shared her outlook, she retained the social responsibility developed earlier. If, on the other hand, her marriage meant moving into a community with values quite different from Vassar's, she was more likely to fall back on the sort of values she had learned *before* going to college.

If a college is to encourage social responsibility, it must (as a minimum) run its own affairs according to values that are known to, and worthy of emulation by its students. The extraordinary thing is how often this minimum requirement is lacking in colleges and universities today, perhaps especially in universities. In these large institutions, students seldom are confronted directly with models of the responsibility we would like them to develop; and faculty members seldom demonstrate for them a sense of loyalty to the purposes of the whole institution.

Rarely are students told what the purpose of their education is, or even that they should seek a purpose. Usually the message they get is "You had better look out for yourself." Most of the appeals and demands are addressed to self-interest, and most of the promised rewards are put in terms of self-satisfaction through success in some vocation or profession. Seldom are students told they should do something because they are going to be leaders of a society that expects important things of them.

Students have little chance to feel that they are capable of giving anything to anybody else. In today's high-pressure system their problem is to survive, and if one is barely surviving, he naturally will have some difficulty in thinking of himself as a person who can lead others and give to others. For most students, being in college means capitulating to a kind of voluntary servitude, and it is quite a jump from that condition to one of socially responsible leadership.

Our goal is to expand both the intellect and the area of motive and feeling, and to bring the two together in a larger whole. To this end we try to mobilize the student's deeper needs and emotions in the interest of intellectual strivings, and at the same time we try to bring intellect to bear upon the issues he cares most deeply about. Once the student is aroused by social and political issues, he needs not only the support of a sympathetic group but confidence in his own thought, judgment, and decision making—a confidence born only of practice. Instead of trying to avoid controversial issues, a college ought to promote analysis of them, including such conflicts of campus life as a student-administration struggle about rules or a faculty-trustees struggle about academic freedom.

I think again of the professor who tried to interest us in issues of the 1920s. In his course, we were supposed to study contemporary Supreme Court cases, which would then be presented in class. Although my friends and I did not have time to read many of the cases, and sometimes used that class to prepare for the next one, our teacher managed somehow to convey to us the importance of his subject. We were impressed by the way that he refused to give up on us, by his assumption that sooner or later we would have to be interested in those great issues, and by his implied faith that we were, though still young and ignorant, the best hope of the nation.

Nowadays, of course, we dismiss from college young people who will not prepare their cases. In my day we did not have to worry about that possibility, for we had been given to understand that society was depending on us to take up many of its tasks. As a matter of fact, as soon as I was through with matters that really were pressing in college, I began to read material of the sort that our teacher offered, and I found it very interesting. What occurs to me now is that he should have used more concrete imagery to convey what the cases really meant. We did not have a clue, for example, about the meaning of labor relations, because we had no reliable images of labor, much less of its relations. Lacking any direct experience, we found the cases abstract and, aside from our persistent teacher, easy to ignore.

Many college students suffer not only from ignorance of the larger world but also from a lack of opportunities to be of service. Fearful of appearing "soft" or unsophisticated, and required to compete successfully with others and to find ways of "beating the system," they pass up chances to be helpful, thus generating a good measure of self-contempt. As this feeling toward the self builds up, some seek an opportunity to sacrifice themselves in some action of great significance; and if they find no action of sufficient import, their unease increases. College students whom we think of as "uncommitted" or "alienated" often seem to be in this situation, and they can even make a correct intellectual analysis of themselves and their trouble without its doing any good.

Possibly the only cure for self-contempt is an actual experience of being helpful, which often can best be had in some radically different setting. Although this experience sooner or later should be connected with or become a part of the student's intellectual life, I avoid suggesting that the only way to educate people to social responsibility is to involve them in social action right now. We know too little about the relationships between the patterns of college behavior and future performances in the world. Vassar women who became leaders in the community were not, in general, campus leaders, nor were they particularly active on the social front as students. In some cases students who are suppressed the most in college may even become radicals later on by striving for the freedom denied to them earlier. Furthermore, premature commitment to some patterns of social action can easily interfere with education.

In general, however, the development of full social responsibility requires experience in social action, or in actions helpful to other people. A young person needs this experience in order to test the adequacy of his judgment, to familiarize himself with the limits of what he can do, and, above all, to learn about the self-fulfillment that comes from being of service to others.

9

Motivation
for Academic
Achievement

Earlier I have taken issue with those who would exalt academic achievement as the sole aim of higher education, particularly when that achievement is defined narrowly by performance in a specialized area and measured even more narrowly by a grade-point average. However, when seen in its broader context as one facet of the student's developing personality, academic achievement can be very important as an indicator of his present level of development and as a stimulus to further development. In this chapter I discuss some of the factors that contribute to high academic achievement and present case-study material on four students who reached this same goal by quite diverse motivational roads.

During our research at Vassar, Donald Brown (1962) developed an "educational typology" based on studies of alumnae. In addition to the *High Achievers,* he found *Over-Achievers,* who earned high grades more by compulsive effort than by a serious appreciation of the intellectual life; *Under-Achievers,* who enjoyed college and grew intellectually without becoming seriously involved in academic work; another group whose college years were marked primarily by *Social Activity* and

Peer-Group Orientation; and finally, *Seekers of Identity,* who were primarily seeking to adjust to a social world radically different from the one they had known. Of these five types, we are here discussing only the first: the students who consistently earn high grades, have an interest in a subject or a field of knowledge deep enough that they are carried along by its demands, and are headed in hopes and in reality for a life of scholarly or professional activity. My definition thus excludes not only the student who labors long and well to submit an *A* thesis in sociology and then goes off to a job as junior partner in his father's business or as typist in an advertising agency, but also the imaginative, erratic student who loves to play with ideas, switching happily from drama to philosophy to science, and who earns some top grades now and then by virtue of scintillating performances.

High academic achievement is sustained variously by dispositions deep in the personality or by social factors that encourage the individual to achieve even though he may not have earlier shown a "drive" to do so. I would like to focus here not on the social inducements but on the factors underlying an individual's disposition to achieve. The following case studies of four girls from the research sample at Vassar offer a glimpse of the kinds of psychological households in which achievement drive is to be found. This is intended not as a formal typology of achievers or as an exhaustive list of types that may exist, but simply as an illustration of the diverse sources of achievement.

Shirley A. made Phi Beta Kappa in her junior year and won an attractive fellowship for graduate study in the humanities. She is a genuine scholar who likes to dig deeply for the determinants behind events and to ponder about the inner meaning of what she observes; she is caught up in the discipline of her subject so that she is led on by its demands and wonders whether she can ever learn enough about it. She makes meaningful and durable personal relationships, both with peers and with people older than she; and her modesty, sensitivity, and reliability stand out even on short acquaintance. She seems to have acquired long ago a sense of direction or of fundamental identity, which permits her to tolerate a considerable amount of conscious conflict and to try diverse alternative roads to her objectives. In the summer after her junior year, before she knew what was happening, she almost married an insistent young man who was already settled in business, but she realized that marriage then would be out of keeping with her general plans.

Both of Shirley's parents placed high value upon education and culture. The father had earned a degree in engineering and became a business executive; the mother, a high school graduate, had worked as a bookkeeper before her marriage. Both read widely, were interested in music and the theater, and entertained literary and artistic people in their home. They were disappointed that their older daughters did not turn out to be outstanding or persistent scholars. For Shirley they had high hopes and expectations. She was a scholar of sorts even when she was very young, spending a great deal of time alone with her books and her thoughts, and she found that good work in school was warmly rewarded by her teachers and her parents. This pattern held all the way through the two progressive elementary schools and the large public scondary school that she attended.

College has been very satisfying for her, especially in the academic sphere. Although reluctant to "bother" faculty members with her problems, she has found in them adequate encouragement, support, friendship, and models for emulation. Oriented primarily toward her family, the faculty, and a few friends with backgrounds and outlooks not unlike her own, she has been almost altogether free of the student peer culture.

As we would expect, her difficulties have had to do with overconscientiousness and with dependence-independence conflicts centered on her family. She had to learn the hard way that she could not keep everything in order, read everything assigned, or do everything an able student might be expected to do. Her concern for "not hurting anyone," which made it hard for her to avoid marriage even after she knew it was not right for her, also made it difficult for her to change roommates, enlarge the circle of her acquaintances, and overcome the shyness and social narrowness with which she began. She has had to struggle not to be intolerant of students who do not share her values or high standards. Most significantly, her very closeness to and identification with her parents, which has been basic to her stability of character and identity since childhood, has intensified the problems of independence. Shirley is aware of these problems, however, and thinks that during her college years she has gradually made progress toward their solution.

During the first twelve years of *Julie B.'s* life, her mother was ill a great deal of the time, and Julie grew close to her father, a farmer with little education and an easy-going nature. She developed a strong interest in the outdoors and in horses and became a strong-minded, competitive girl who could dominate her older brother. She admired most in her father the fact that he was "always even-tempered and considerate without losing any of his masculinity."

After twelve, she says, she "somehow left Daddy behind." She began increasingly to share her mother's interests in music, literature, and the other arts. The mother was a teacher and had planned to go back to the university as soon as she got her children into school, and eventually she did go back. She regularly got after her husband for being too easy-going. He went his quiet way, not minding that his wife and daughter had highbrow tastes and interests, even admiring them for it, but he did not undertake to imitate them.

Julie, now a senior, arrived at college with the intention of becoming a serious scholar, and she has stuck to it. Her interests in the outdoors, in athletics, even in horses, have been maintained, but they have not competed seriously with her work. She is conscience-stricken if an assignment is not completed and feels she must not in any circumstances permit her grade-point average to slip. She has found models, and warm friends and supporters, among the faculty, while remaining more or less alienated from the great majority of her fellow students, who do not share her deep intellectual commitments.

When Julie was a freshman, the research staff presented her interview data, without interpretation, to a group of psychiatrists, psychologists, and sociologists. She was the staff's idea of a really promising student, but the conferees kept asking, "What's wrong with her?" They thought she would need psychotherapy. Major concerns were her overconscientiousness and her relative lack of interest in conventional feminine roles. As for the latter, she is already married to a graduate student in science. Although she remains overly conscientious, this form of behavior will probably find its niche in the atmosphere of a graduate school.

Connie C. is her father's daughter. He is an intellectual lawyer who, implicitly, has counted on his daughter's becoming a serious scholar. The mother is a high school graduate and a homemaker with social interests. Connie thinks that she was close to her mother until she was about four, when her brother was born. After that, she preferred and felt closer to her father. She raised dogs, preferred dungarees to dresses, and went in for gardening. Her special delight was working on projects with her father.

As a freshman in college she made an honest attempt to please her mother and to achieve some comfort in middle-class feminine roles. But the people she admired most were Newton, Einstein, and Machiavelli, and she felt that "Women should do more than a lot of married women do, whose state is one of existing rather than growing."

The college years have been marked by much conflict with her mother and by movement toward a conception of herself as a scientist and an independent person, which has involved much self-analysis and the painful process of giving up her original friends and finding new ones. The faculty have remained distant, but in some cases admired, figures; she has found among them models of intellectual women, and both men and women who appreciated her worth as a scholar.

But her troubles are not over. She is a major in natural science, as was her intention when she arrived in college, and here she feels external pressure to attend to what she calls the "recipe" (and what her father calls the "grub") aspects of science, while her strong inclination is to concentrate on its conceptual and theoretical aspects. She is a systematic thinker of rare quality, but she will have trouble finding roles in life that will permit the full exercise of these talents.

Sally D. is the one of our group of high achievers whose motivations are in large part "neurotic." Her parents were divorced when she was two years old and both soon remarried. She lived first with one parent and then with the other, finally settling in her teens with her father. Her mother attended college for two years, and is described by Sally as a member of "the Canasta set" who leads an "empty life—stupid, petty, ignorant, hypochondriacal." The father is an artist and a college graduate. He is described as intelligent, erudite, preoccupied. Sally has felt that, although he was kind to her, he did not have faith in her ability or serious purposes.

Feeling rejected by both parents, she took it out on the world in a variety of imaginative ways. As a private-school girl she was brilliant, and this trait now appears to be durable. Since the day she arrived at college, she has been focused on the faculty, "the only people worth knowing." She has had a succession of faculty favorites, now of one sex and now of the other, but she has always had a few very close friends who shared her interest in the faculty and her contempt for the vast majority of her fellow students.

She loves the gossip and little conspiracies of the campus, and is privy to all kinds of special information about the inner life of the college. It was touch and go whether she would remain in college through her freshman year, but she gradually grew to admire certain women teachers and to feel that she, too, would become a college teacher. In time she fully incorporated the values and ways of the faculty. It is a fairly safe bet that she will take a Ph.D. in English and become a good college teacher.

There is no doubt that she has used her relations with the faculty to work out problems that have persisted in her family relationships since childhood. Most fundamental, it seems, is an identification with her father, which is based on frustration, hostility, and fear, and a closeness to women, which counteracts strong elements of contempt for them and for herself. Although she might benefit from psychotherapy, she shows no inclination to seek it. The fact that her education has been "neurotically" motivated does not make her any the less educated, nor does it necessarily diminish the value of her intellectual activity. It might even, in fact, enhance her contribution.

Although these four students do not necessarily represent all the patterns of high achievement that are to be found among women in college, it is of some interest to note what they have in common. We might in this way arrive at hypotheses worthy of being tested with larger populations.

In all four cases one or the other of the parents was highly educated, or placed high value upon scholarly attainments, and held high hopes and expectations for the daughter. In all four cases there was early, close involvement with the parents and early and persistent awkwardness in social relations with peers. With Sally D. of course, the parental involvement was negative, but even in her case there has been a persistent orientation toward parents and other adults rather than toward peers. In the cases of Shirley, Julie, and Connie there was early and very genuine internalization of parental standards and values. One might say that these girls were already inner-directed even as young children, and the important events of their lives were already taking place inside themselves. Hence we find them spending much time alone.

In all four cases the drive toward academic achievement has more than one source; its determination is complex. One could go some distance toward explaining it as emulation of, or desire to please, one or both parents or parent substitutes, rather than on the basis that girls naturally tend to carry on in the tradition of their families. But in each case it seems that special tensions were generated by early relations with the parents, and early emotional drives were channeled into the scholarship motive. Yet this channelization could hardly have occurred had not one or the other parent represented intellectual values.

Oriented primarily toward the faculty, all four of these students remained outside, and were little influenced by, the dominant student culture. One might ask how such students as these would have fared in a college environment where the student and faculty cultures were essentially the same, with the students in general oriented toward serious scholarship. They might have been happier as students, but whether they would have developed as fully, or grown to know themselves and their true values as well, is another question.

Except for Sally D. there is an aspect of slow maturation. Perhaps this impression is given primarily by their persisting dependence on parents and on other adults, and by their willingness to accept discipline. How much should we worry about this? It is our impression that these students as graduating seniors are particularly open to further growth—in fact, to more or less indefinitely continuing growth—possibly because they have still to accomplish certain developmental tasks such as establishing autonomy, which many people of their age already have behind them. But it seems they started out as if destined to go a long way, and took time to consolidate each gain before beginning a new undertaking. Perhaps this pattern of development is associated with the type of early closeness to the parents that has been described.

What is the basis for our saying that Sally D.'s motivations were neurotic or, more properly, that her motivations are significantly more neurotic than those of the others? The distinction is not easy to make. There was, after all, some excuse for the psychiatrists' supposing that Julie B. would need psychotherapy; and Shirley A.'s fear that she might hurt someone has the earmarks of a neurotic symptom. It is tempting to say that all four of the girls had childhood neuroses, from which the first three more or less recovered.

The ways in which Sally D. differs from the others seem only quantitative. The strains upon her as a child were more severe; the areas of her personality dominated by unconscious conflicts are broader; and her scholarship is more largely a means for solving personality problems, less an end in itself. One qualitative difference stands out. Sally's is the only case in which identification with parents involves large elements of hostility and fear; in all the other cases the parent(s) "taken inside," or incorporated into the self, was loving and worthy.

Calling attention to ways in which these high achievers are alike is not the same as saying what distinguishes them from students who are not high achievers. We all know some students who seemed, at the time they entered college, like those described here, but who shortly adapted themselves to student society, learned the joys of social life, and contented themselves with ordinary academic performances. Another type who resembles the high achiever even later in her college career is the conscientious, hard-working winner of high grades who gives up serious intellectual activity as soon as she graduates from college—the type Donald Brown and other researchers have called "over-achievers." There is some evidence that these young women are solidly identified with their mothers, who are pushing their daughters toward educational achievement but who were not themselves serious scholars or even unambiguously in favor of their daughters becoming scholars of the sort described above.

In order to identify potential high achievers, we need to elaborate and test the sort of typology proposed by Brown. Within college however, we can count less on altering basic dispositions than on providing challenge, inducements, and support. One kind of support apparently crucial to potential high achievers is access to at least a few admired faculty members and to an "outgroup" apart from the otherwise dominant peer culture.

10

Education
for
Creativity

Is education for creativity different from good general education? On one side of this question, a case can be made for special schools for highly talented people. Giannini (1966), for example, has recently given a glowing account of a music school in which the young people happily turn to such subjects as English and History after first being given the whole morning for study and practice in the musical specialty they have chosen. Heist (1966) and Snyder (1966) have also suggested that potentially creative students are rather special and might very well need a special kind of education. On the other hand, MacKinnon (1966), in considering what might be done to develop creativity within a program of general education, has proposed that students need a certain amount of structure in their environments, as well as broad experience and models of how to use their culture in order to free, or to find expression for, their impulses.

No doubt all of these things would be good for highly talented or potentially creative people, but would they not be good for all young people? MacKinnon's suggestions, moreover, have much in common with those offered in Chapter 8, on the development of social responsibility. In this connection it is interesting to note the finding of Heist (1966) that, despite striking exceptions, "potential creativity" and social responsibility in college students are positively correlated. I would say, then, that education for creativity has much in common with good education in general. Education traditionally has meant a "leading forth" of potentialities. Its aim is to develop the whole person as fully as possible, to make him increasingly human and unafraid of diversity. This is very different from training, which tends to make people more alike, perhaps not so much in music as in science and the professions, where persons have to learn common techniques, attitudes, values, and styles of work, as well as the language of the field. There is, of course, some interaction between educational and training procedures. Many young people, when they make a decision as to what they are going to do, begin to define themselves in terms of their discipline. This is sometimes quite valuable developmentally, for it may supply a much needed sense of self. But, in general, there is a certain amount of tension between the two kinds of procedures. Most undergraduate teachers in our colleges today are interested in recruiting students into their discipline as early as possible and professionalizing them thoroughly—a process that tends to warp education and should thus be postponed until graduate school.

Turning now to creativity, it seems to me that we should differentiate between creativity as a durable characteristic of personality and such creative acts as finding novel solutions to problems or new ways of posing them. In the background of this meaningful novelty, there is usually a diversity of experience, a wide assortment of mental images, which are there, as it were, to be connected. Creative behavior depends not only upon a durable state of affairs in the person but upon the situation in which a person works and upon the times in which he lives. Many people who achieved a great reputation for creativity were lucky. They came along at a time when there was a readiness in society for just those things they wanted to do. Other people are extraordinarily unlucky, being so far ahead of their times, or so offbeat, that their creative productivity leads to no recognition either by colleagues or by the general public. A psychologist who wanted to study race relations in 1950, for example, would have found it extremely hard to get support, except from a few farsighted groups such as the Society for the Psychological Study of Social Issues. After 1954 research on race relations became very fashionable, and a great deal of creative behavior has recently been shown. Another situational factor of great importance is the kind of discipline in which the person works. In a "consensual" discipline (such as chemistry, which the general public finds useful and nonthreatening) a researcher finds support more easily than a worker in a "dissensual" discipline, such as social science or fine arts, which is still widely mistrusted (Pinner, 1962; see also Chapter 3). Different kinds of people are recruited to these two kinds of discipline (Bereiter and Freedman, 1962), and quite possibly different kinds of underlying personality structures lead to good work in them.

A number of writers, including MacKinnon (1966), Heist (1966), and Snyder (1966), have spoken of a personality syndrome often found in creative people. MacKinnon (1966) has used the term *creativity* to refer to a cluster of traits, including flexibility of thinking, breadth of perspective, autonomy, self-awareness, openness to experience, breadth of interests, and freedom of impulse, which when independently measured are found not only to go together but to differentiate highly creative adults from less creative ones. Ravenna Helson (1966) has described a group of artistic, imaginative college women, some of them creative and some not. She describes an "artistic-imaginative" syndrome common among creative people, but which by itself is not enough to lead to creative work, and concludes that a drive for accomplishment and an element of "masculinity" in the makeup must also be present.

The artistic-imaginative syndrome, Helson found, embodies "impulsivity" and "investment in inner life," which are signs of impulse expression. Helson's results accord well with the theory that some kind of contact between a person's conscious ego and his unconscious processes is important in most kinds of creative work. If people have this kind of access to their inner selves and are able to use it in their writing or artistic productions, then we should expect that their impulses will find expression in other areas as well.

"Masculinity" as measured by Helson—largely a matter

of freedom from a narrow and conventional "feminine" self-conception—increases in women during the college years. Impulse freedom and all the other traits which MacKinnon says distinguish creative people also increase during college in both women and men (see Chapter 2). This is a point of great importance; for it follows that—given some amount of talent, perhaps no more than is to be found in the average person—we have the opportunity, even as late as college, to develop creative potential through education.

This opportunity may vary from one field of work to another. It seems that creativity in literature or psychology or social science is a rather different thing from creativity in music, art, mathematics, and perhaps in those natural sciences that depend heavily on mathematics. Talent in the latter fields is displayed relatively early in the individual's life, and its expression does not seem to require a wide range of experience. To make a contribution in natural science a man must, of course, first provision himself with a great deal of specialized knowledge, but, even so, a physicist can still produce creatively when in his early twenties—a feat more difficult for a psychologist, who must have not only *knowledge about* human behavior but a genuine *acquaintance with* it.

It is noteworthy that a number of creative people in psychology have had quite diverse backgrounds. Edward Tolman, for example, studied engineering before he discovered psychology. Freud was first a physiologist; he did very precise experimental work before he became a practicing physician, which led him to become a psychoanalyst, his third career. Most of all, he loved speculative thought and would have preferred to be a philosopher. The kind of diversity of background that we find in Freud might well be just the thing to supply that breadth and richness of experience that a person needs to make new connections among ideas. The big question is when to give the training that is necessary to the performance of many tasks in our society. Education may be impaired by training, but can we afford to postpone the training until the graduate years? When we think of one of our own sons, would we be willing to let everything remain open-ended until he went to graduate school, where he would begin his training, or would we begin to become anxious about his career while he was still in high school?

For example, if we were thinking about his becoming a physicist, would we, like his teachers, want to be sure that he took plenty of mathematics in high school so that he would be well prepared for all those courses that are said to depend upon it?

It has often been said that if we want to develop musical talent we must start people when they are young and require them to work hard. Physicists sometimes try to persuade us that it is the same with their science, and some chemists would like to identify talent for chemistry even in elementary school children and to start grooming them for chemistry then and there. We know that there is much pressure on young persons to reach their choice of chemistry in high school so that they can be sure to have those courses which are considered fundamental to later development in this field. Why not schools for chemists then—like the music school described by Giannini? Indeed there is a tendency in our society to do for the natural sciences what has long been done for music and ballet: identifying talent early and preparing it rigorously. In some fields of science, research is even being orchestrated.

There is a value conflict here between the need to produce people who can make specific contributions to society and the need to develop individuals as fully as possible. Perhaps all we can do is to recognize these conflicting values and try to arrange things so that if one is realized fully it will be at as little expense to the other as possible. At Bowdoin College all seniors, who now live together in the Senior Center, are required to take two seminars outside their major field of study. Many who are fully committed to careers in science enjoy getting as far away from their specialties as possible, and they enjoy close association with students in different fields. It is very doubtful that their careers in science will be hurt by this experience. They might, indeed, be helped. Why not, then, require three seminars outside the major, or since most of what is taught in the senior year will probably be taught again in graduate school, permit only one course *within* the major?

Premature specialization may harm not only the developing individual but the discipline in which he works. In the study of human life or society, precosity in the use of concepts and methods may easily serve as a substitute for experience, and even as a defense against it, thus blocking creativity at its source. We can see this in psychology, where, due to the continuing "upgrading" of the undergraduate curriculum, an increasing number of entering graduate students arrive with a good grasp of certain methods and a conception of themselves as scientists but with little background for judging what the problems are. They are then so taken up with empirical busywork that they have little chance to acquire introspective knowledge or vital acquaintance with the field. The result could easily be a narrow, mechanistic psychology whose applications consisted in the manipulation of people.

It is sad to see the same thing happening in humanistic studies. Such is the domination of the university by a conceptual and methodological orientation that a college bookstore may now display fewer literary productions than books of criticism. Thus Enright (1966) could recently write:

> As a pupil of mine, by no means abnormally lazy, corrupt, intelligent, or witty, said recently: "I have followed your lectures on *Macbeth* and I have read the criticism. Do I have to read the play as well?"

Probably the fields that Pinner (1966) calls dissensual are harmed more by premature or obsessive book learning than are the consensual ones, though it may be doubted that physics or math loses more by precosity than music does. One is tempted to say to the physicist that we will give him high school if he will give us college, but probably we should set as our goal the intensification of human experience at both stages.

We should not, of course, leave the impression that productive creativity serves society but not the individual. It may be that if we provide the conditions for creativity as self-fulfillment, the needs of society would be well enough taken care of. Creativity in this sense may be found not only in science, the professions, or "high culture" but wherever the individual has a chance to express himself; and in a culture where it flourishes, we find that the ordinary things of life have aesthetic value. Probably everyone has some potential for creativity of this kind, and none should be denied the opportunity for an education that can nourish it.

Another reason why I argue that education for creativity is essentially the same as good general education has to do with the difficulty of identifying in school those who may some day be creative. Heist (1966) goes to considerable length to show how tenuous such predictions are, and he cautions against stereotyping this group of students. Even if they do have much in common and can be differentiated from other young people, there are probably many potentially creative college students who have not yet shown any signs of what they can some day do. If we cannot be sure which people should have special attention, then the safest course is to see to it that everybody in college receives as good as we have to offer.

In considering this kind of general education, I make use of the theoretical model developed in previous chapters. Before considering its implications for creativity, however, I must point out that other people have quite different models, including some that are rarely made explicit. One dominant model in American higher education was suggested by a lawyer who wrote me a letter critical of our book *The American College* (Sanford, 1962). Apparently a conservative man, he said that this rather dull-looking volume was actually a revolutionary document in that it sought to implement the "liberal bias." He wished, however, to give us credit for one thing. "I used to think that education was to learning what food is to eating," he said. "I see now that that is not so." This model, that education is to learning as food is to eating, is widespread in the United States, and many people are guided by it even though they never quite say so.

When education is conceived of as a matter of teaching facts, then the "explosion of knowledge" means that more facts need to be taught. Since we have few means for integrating knowledge, or perhaps do not even believe in it, courses and departments proliferate amid a general feeling that our primary need is for more and more efficient means for teaching facts. Students who adapt themselves to this system begin to conceive of themselves as fragmented, and even to engage in the business of fragmenting others.

The rise of technological aids to education was made

possible by the existence of the behavioristic model; and the wide-spread acceptance and use of these aids tend to sustain the model. Mechanized means for teaching facts are sometimes introduced with the idea of freeing the teacher for more important work, but the aids cost money, and investment in them exerts a strong pressure to use them maximally. Add to this the fact that many teachers cannot think of anything more important than teaching the facts of their own disciplines, and we have constant reinforcement of the be-havioristic model.

It should not be surprising that we now have on our hands something of a rebellion against the narrowly cognitive ac-cent in education. Twelve or fourteen years of emotionally barren and often meaningless fact-grubbing seems to leave a person starved for feelings and for symbols. One form the rebellion has taken is the LSD movement, in which people seek the instant provision of what has been omitted from all the years of formal education. Alpert and Cohen (1966) tell of a boy who had taken LSD but was disap-pointed and complained that he had seen no such visions as Aldous Huxley had described. When he added that it was probably because Huxley had taken mescalin, one of the authors could not resist tell-ing the boy that there was a greater difference between him and Huxley than between LSD and mescalin. Emotion and the symbolic functions, like other aspects of the person, have to be developed through education. We are left, however, with the persistent ques-tion of whether there is not some way in which young people suffer-ing from earlier repression can be opened to genuine experience and thus to valuable self-modification—a process comparable to psycho-therapy but much quicker. There is evidence that some patients may benefit from LSD if a proper administration of the drug is followed by psychotherapeutic procedures for maintaining the openness to experience that has been achieved (Fadiman, 1965). But it seems that young pople who are disposed to use drugs such as LSD for kicks are already too open, in the sense that impulse expression has run ahead of development in the ego.

The problem here is like that posed by the "potential creatives" described by Heist (1966)—students who have creative productions to their credit and who are complex, high on impulse expression, low on authoritarianism, and have difficulty accepting the regimen of a college. These young people seem to have been exposed to too much, too early: they have already had experiences which people now middle-aged postponed until graduate school. People of this latter generation may be forgiven their nostalgia for the days when students arrived at college fresh from the hills or plains, ready to seek and find and be amazed. We do not see many students like this today. Most arrive at college already bearing the stigmata of our mass culture as well as of the academic precosity described above. Amid the fact-mania that seems to have taken hold of many schools, some educational psychologists seem to be arguing today that anything can be learned by anybody at any time and that the earlier in the individual's life we get on with it, the better. More and more of the traditional college curriculum is being taught in high school and the high school curriculum in elementary school; the time may come when everybody will know everything, but nobody will understand anything.

In thinking of potentially creative but unorganized young people, we may take some heart from the fact of individual differences in rates of development. Some of these people may yet find themselves, some while they are still in college. After they have become organized, they may look back on their present state as a manifestation of growing pains. They may be contrasted with the group of students who have not shown any creativity yet, but who under certain conditions and proper stimulation might begin to bloom later on. Students' confusion about what to do with themselves is lasting longer and longer. Katz (1966) and Keniston (1966) have recently called attention to the fact that this kind of confusion or uncertainty is quite common among senior men. Although this is no doubt due in part to confusion in our society, the period of exposure to varieties of experience is lasting longer now. There is probably more tolerance for taking time to find oneself than there was during the 1950s, when the pressure was on young people to hurry up and decide on their careers. It is somewhat unnerving to encounter seniors who are still up in the air about what to do with themselves, but if we consider the times in which we live and if we have the right kind of developmental perspective, we need not be driven to panic. My inclination is to believe that most of these seniors will find themselves, if somebody will still have faith in them. If we insist on a system that eliminates or refuses admission to all who have not found themselves at the right time, then of course we are in serious trouble. A developmental perspective should help us to see that people who take a long time to get organized are often the very ones who go far in the long run.

Consideration of potentially creative students is one basis for criticism of what the colleges have been doing. Heist (1966) has shown that a majority of these students, even in the highly selective liberal-arts institutions, do not stay to finish the course. There is no evidence that the neglect of these students is due to the fact that others are getting more than their share of attention.

Fundamental to reform in the colleges is a change of attitude on the part of the people who run them. The faculty must take some interest in general education and begin to conceive of themselves as educators. Unless a higher proportion of faculty become interested in students, eager to know some of them and willing to do something for them, nothing much is going to happen. But most teachers on our campuses today are not interested in discussing education and are not well informed about it. It is still true—or at least it was until the student protest at Berkeley—that most university teachers would regard it as dangerous to their careers to show any genuine interest in students: colleagues would soon accuse them of such deviations as "putting students ahead of subjects," or attempting to turn the campus into a therapeutic community. Snyder (1966) tells the story of a student who was referred to the psychiatric service because, though he seemed very bright, he was falling far behind in a math course. It turned out that instead of merely applying the formulas as all the others were doing, he insisted on deriving them for himself because he could not accept them from authorities. Any college teacher should be able to take note of such problems, find out what the trouble is, and have some idea of a remedy.

In order to support a change of attitude among teachers, the colleges and universities must reform their reward system instead of relying merely on adjustments in the methods of formal instruction. Nobody knows how the reform can be brought about, but surely we must begin by recognizing how serious and deep-seated the problem is. Some suggestions about how to begin are offered below and also in Chapters 14 and 18.

A major contribution to educational reform is the "Muscatine Report."* It begins with a stirring description and analysis of the situation of today's university students and ends with forty-two recommendations for change at Berkeley. Seen in historical perspective, the report is a great achievement. Ten years ago, no one who talked about students in this way would have been listened to in academic circles. An enormous gain has been made in raising the level of faculty discussion of education. Many of us are just now learning how to discuss educational problems; and the report, in showing us how to do this and in encouraging us to do it, has made a signal contribution.

Having said this, I can state what in my view is wrong with the report. It does not go far enough. It flirts with the developmental point of view, but it does not really take it to heart. The authors are willing to recognize that students are human beings who, like everybody else, need to be shown a few acts of kindness occasionally, but I am afraid that the authors are really not convinced that learning itself is a highly personal thing, a *human* process integral with all the other functions of the whole person. It is one thing to be kind to students being put through the mechanical business of learning content by rote; something else to look on them as people who learn the way the rest of us do—painfully, in response to challenge, and with all of our selves.

If we look at education as individual development, and are really serious about it, then all kinds of possibilities become open. In regard to these possibilities, the report does not go far enough. This is, of course, quite understandable. It would be easier to design a new institution on the basis of what we now know about education than to modify according to plan an enormous and complicated structure such as the University of California at Berkeley. Recom-

* A report of the Select Committee on Education of the Academic Senate of the University of California, Berkeley, under the chairmanship of Professor Charles Muscatine (Academic Senate, 1966).

mendations for reform are made on the basis of shrewd judgments not of what would be ideal but of what the traffic will bear. Had the report been based on the idea of education as a developmental process, it would have had to consider ways and means for de-emphasizing the learning of academic content. It would have made much of the point that different contents may be used to achieve the same developmental end. This is the beginning of educational reform. It is not how much students are offered in the way of courses and syllabi that matters; it is the experiences they have.

When we look at the problem in this way, it becomes obvious that the "explosion in knowledge" carries no great message for educators. Since we can never teach more than fragments of all the knowledge there is, we should make our choices on the basis of what we believe the student needs in order to change him as a person. The report admits that quite different contents will do. It praises the Tussman program, which assumes that intensive study of Greek civilization may be as good for freshmen as the study of five elementary courses in as many different fields (see Chapters 4 and 15). If the report had only taken the next step and directly challenged the departmental structure, at least as it determines the curriculum for freshmen and sophomores, we would be well on the way to educational reform—provided we could find teachers willing to devote themselves to the lower division.

As matters stand, most of the really valuable things that we think need doing have to be added to what is already being done. At Stanford we introduced freshman seminars in the fall of 1965, and within the year this program became one of the most generally applauded features of Stanford education. It became possible not because of departmental initiative or eagerness to cooperate, but only because of a gift that could be used in any way that an *ad hoc* committee thought favorable to creativity. There is nobody to tell the departments what to do. Until this changes, we are not likely to have deep-going reform at Berkeley or at any other institution of higher learning. We cannot expect the faculty to teach everything they are supposed to teach for their departments during the day and then in their spare time and out of the goodness of their hearts give a freshman seminar.

If the attitudes that I advocate were adopted, it would not be necessary for the report to be so faint-hearted in its recommendations about grading. It is not at all revolutionary today to conceive of all grading on the pass-fail basis, yet the report restricts itself to allowing students only one pass-fail course each term. This is probably as far as the faculty now would go, but it would not be surprising if within the next few years distinguished undergraduate institutions were to give all their courses on a pass-fail basis. It will be recognized, in time, that what students need for their education is not grades of the usual sort but criticism of their work.

To ask a college teacher to be aware of the changing needs of students, and to be on hand to meet the needs of particular students, is, of course, to ask a great deal. This is individual education, of the sort that is ordinarily found only at a few expensive colleges. Yet we need not be discouraged about the possibilities of realizing some of the benefits of that system in large institutions. For one thing, increasing knowledge of personality development in students and of the meaning of student-faculty relationships may become increasingly a part of faculty culture, so that it may influence the day-to-day behavior of the faculty member. Much will depend on our ability to produce literature about students that is sufficiently interesting and well written that the faculty member can ignore it only with difficulty.

Again, it is well to remember that what matters is not the frequency or the duration of student-faculty encounters but their quality. I have heard both students and faculty recount instances in which a few minutes of communication, in the right circumstances, sufficed to change the student's life. A show of personal interest at a time when the student is in special need of it, or a show of firmness when this is clearly in the student's interest, takes little time and could become a natural occurrence in a faculty-student community; it may be of crucial importance to the student's development.

It is well to remember, too, that most undergraduates are not looking for intimate relationships with faculty. Many, including some of the best ones, have guilt feelings and are afraid of being found out. We are not likely to be overwhelmed by students in need of intimacy. There is no call for us to have relationships of equality and good fellowship with students, and there is little to be gained from our seeking students out in order to meet *our* needs—for popularity, for freedom from guilt, and the like. What *is* called for is an arrangement of academic life that will make it possible for students and faculty to get at each other, to reveal themselves to each other, so that the truly beneficial brief encounters can occur—this, and the sort of outlook that I have spoken of earlier, one that is neither sentimental nor clinical but which embodies a decent concern for the student as a human being for whose development the faculty has some responsibility.

If we can free college teachers from their preoccupation with covering content, free undergraduate education from its domination by the departments, and free all concerned from the tyranny of grades, we can get back to a fundamental principle of pedagogy: helping students to go from their own experiences, from the examination of empirical phenomena, to the generation of concepts. In many areas of inquiry, such as philosophy, literature, history, and political science, this means making use of original sources instead of subjecting students to a massive conceptual baggage concocted by professors who needed to write textbooks or prepare lectures. Here we find some of the grimmest testimony to the fact that the typical undergraduate course structure has been made for the faculty rather than for the students. I know of an advanced course in social thought in which the students have to learn various interpretations of Hobbes contributed by the teacher and his friends and colleagues—prolific writers all—but have no chance to get at Hobbes himself. Probably more than a few readers of this book have had psychology courses in which we read and were told a great deal *about* Freud but were never assigned the original. I was led to read Freud by a teacher who denounced him in terms so scathing that it aroused my curiosity— and my interest in the forbidden.

Teachers of the physical and biological sciences have, of course, known for a long time how to use the laboratory as a means for keeping concepts tied to observable phenomena, but the neglect of this principle in the social sciences is distressing. The study of social science ought to begin, it seems to me, in the field, and students ought to be discouraged from trafficking in concepts unconnected with observations. It is gratifying to note that the Muscatine Report recommends, as one possibility, that a problem-centered curriculum be tried with freshmen and sophomores, organized perhaps around urban problems (see Chapter 18).

All of this seems elementary; yet the principle I am speaking of is so badly neglected today that even a small reform along the lines advocated could be labeled a creative approach to education for creativity. One could probably get a foundation grant to support it.

To return now to the special group of potentially creative students discussed above, it seems to me that a little understanding and faith will go a long way. Students, even some fairly rebellious ones, are usually grateful for small favors. After the Berkeley revolt, the deans at Stanford spent a great deal of time listening to students, singly and in delegations, and a few reforms in student life and in the academic realm have been instituted. It would be going too far to say that these measures averted overt rebellion, for probably none was in the offing anyway, but they did help to create a good climate for discussion. The amount and the high level of discussion of education in the Stanford *Daily* during the year following the events at Berkeley was, in my experience, unique. At least some of the potentially creative students undoubtedly had their morale boosted.

Listening to students and being concerned about them does not mean giving them what they say they want. We can expect them to be inconsistent and even contradictory in expressing their wants, and they are not in a good position to know what they need. Protesting students have been accused of having no program, as if they could develop an educational philosophy and educational procedures where their elders have failed. I hope I can complain about my physician, accuse him of indifference, psychological blindness, ignorance, and immaturity without being expected to know what he knows or to be able to tell him how to run his business. At a recent conference on education a panel of students had the task of presenting "the student point of view." When they were through, a dean asked, "What is it that you really want?" A student replied, "It's not up to us to tell you what we want. That would be too cheap a way for you to find out." I think he meant that it is up to educators to understand students, to know what they need and how their needs might be met. What students say they want is *one* basis for inferring their needs, but it can never be the only basis. The educator must know about students in general and have access to a theory of personality development that can guide his selection of instrumentalities. A few indications that we knew what we were about and were devoted to our purposes would go a long way, even with the potentially creative students.

There is no denying that some of these latter students can be difficult. Some are self-destructive and deliberately provocative. As suggested earlier, some have experienced premature gratification of impulses and are in rather desperate need of external control—which they cannot bring themselves to accept. Some of these latter can accept leadership from adults of proven worth who share their own convictions; others reject the whole idea of leadership, even the idea of organized social action. But it is of little help to suggest that individual psychopathology is at work here, and it would be fatal to indicate to these students that on this account their arguments do not deserve to be dealt with on their merits. We have to admit that it has taken some pretty far-out students to call attention to truths that should have been obvious. I suspect that in the future as in the past we will need some extreme deviants to encourage the rank and file to break the bonds of bland conformity.

Student protests from time to time, and a continuing student interest in their own education, can help to bring about those changes in faculty attitudes that I have urged. Although a change in the reward system will be necessary to sustain faculty interests in general education, we must remember that teachers can be appealed to on other bases besides money and status. Some faculty members, for example, can be induced to enter into discussion of their teaching, of their experiences and problems in the classroom and in their relations with students. As Katz and Korn (1966) have demonstrated, this kind of discussion leads to greater awareness of themselves, which is a basis for greater awarenesss of, and hence interest in, the processes of students. Katz and Korn have also shown that faculty members can become interested in research on students through taking part in it themselves. All the teachers responsible for sections of a large elementary course took part in all phases of an inquiry designed to evaluate the course. The course improved before the evaluation was completed. This kind of thing can be done at low cost on a large scale, with benefit to all concerned and without threatening the college teacher's conception of himself as a specialist in a subject.

I believe that the research on students and colleges that has been reported in recent years has had some influence, that it has helped to raise the level of current discussions of higher education, and that good will come of this. But more important, the times are now on the side of educational reform. The immediate postwar years and the period of the 1950s were great times for research and graduate training; practically everybody in the university, with the exception of a few other-worldly humanistic scholars, found a way to use federal funds to strengthen his discipline, upgrade his department, and advance his special research interests. Those were times when professors could say, "This would be a great place if it were not for the students." Student protest movements are, fundamentally, a reflection of changed times, and they are a warning that the colleges and universities must change. We are no longer under great pressure to hurry and produce the manpower to keep the productive machinery of the nation going; rather, we have the task, and the opportunity, to re-examine the nation's purposes. This is what our students want us to do, and this is what they need. We have a chance to rediscover, to restore, and to advance the values of the liberal university. To do so would be to provide a better home for the creativity we admire.

11

Alcohol
Education
in Schools
and Colleges

The title of this chapter will suggest to some readers that they are in for a temperance lecture. There are historical grounds for such a suspicion. State laws requiring the public schools to teach about alcohol were passed, for the most part, in the spirit of Prohibition, and the teaching that followed had as its main object the discouragement of drinking by young people. As late as 1943, according to Roe (1943), textbooks that dealt with the subject of alcohol were still slanted in a temperance direction. But there have been some important changes in alcohol education in the last twenty-five years. Paralleling increases in scientific research, the development of voluntary and public programs for coping with alcohol-related problems, and the spread of enlightenment in society, teaching about alcohol and drinking has become far more objective than it was.

It is still not clear, however, what the youth should be told about drinking: nobody claims that just saying "don't" or dwelling on the dangers of alcohol has the intended effect. The proportion of teen-agers who drink in settings other than their homes is high, and it is common for them to begin when they are as young as thirteen or fourteen. While the viewings with alarm of the daily press may be to some extent discounted, since they represent an effort to satisfy the adult appetite for sensational stories about the doings of youth, there is no denying that alcohol is not infrequently a factor in youthful behavior that is illegal or troublesome or even damaging to the individuals involved. When episodes of this kind are reported, parents become aroused and blame the schools and the police, while representatives of these agencies, not unnaturally, blame the parents. Basic to all this is a persistent ambivalence toward drinking in the culture of a people who treasure the image of the hard-drinking frontiersman, but who also passed the Eighteenth Amendment to the Constitution; a people who now seem to regard drinking as a natural part of everyday life, but who maintain on the books a mass of laws designed to restrict consumption of alcoholic beverages. There is uncertainty about what to tell the youth, because we as a society are not altogether certain about our own behavior and have worked out no generally agreed-upon standards governing the use of alcohol. What we need is an evaluative scheme based on an understanding of the various contexts and meanings of drinking and abstaining, and of their implications for long-range social and individual developmental goals.

To say that teaching about alcohol is more objective than it used to be is to make an inference from limited information. There have been no national surveys of what the schools are doing, of what material is presented or how much or in what manner. What we have are the impressions of experts in alcohol education, who have visited many schools, and the reports of school administrators and teachers concerning programs in particular schools or districts. Such impressions and reports seem to indicate that the prevailing practice today is to devote a limited amount of time to teaching "the facts"—meaning, usually, what is known about the physiological effects of alcohol on the body. Practices vary widely, however, from district to district. In some school systems a prohibitionist point of view still prevails, and students are given dire warnings about the evils of drinking. More common are those systems that do no more than offer a token of compliance with the law by, for example, inviting or allowing an interested outside speaker, usually a temperance man, to address the students. In other states the Departments of Education have laid out comprehensive programs of instruction, with extensive teaching materials based on current knowledge, and some schools make a conscientious effort to have the material taught in the schools, with due attention to what is appropriate for different grades. In some schools facts about the physiological effects of alcohol and biological processes in alcohol addiction are presented in biology courses, and material about the psychology and sociology of drinking is presented in social studies; in addition, as many as 30 hours of teaching about alcohol-related phenomena and problems are provided for in a "problems" course, while counselors are prepared to help students who have special problems, such as an alcoholic parent. Programs of this latter sort are of comparatively recent origin.

Although Alcoholics Anonymous was founded in the mid-1930s, the development of voluntary and public programs for coping with alcohol problems has occurred mainly since 1940. The National Council on Alcoholism (a voluntary organization founded in 1944) and the various state alcoholism programs (of which there are now 40) have been concerned mainly with the treatment of persons suffering from alcoholism, but they also have an interest in the prevention of this condition, an interest that has led them to give some attention to alcohol education in the schools. These agencies or programs are committed to a scientific approach to alcohol problems; for the most part, they employ professional staffs with training in medicine, psychiatry, public health, social welfare, psychology, sociology, or education. As interest in prevention through education has increased over the years, an increasing number of professional people have specialized in alcohol education. The Association for the Advancement of Instruction about Alcohol and Narcotics was founded and began publishing its own journal in 1954. Regional conferences on alcohol education have become fairly common, and institutes for teachers are held every summer in a number of states. These institutes have taken much of their inspiration from the Yale (now Rutgers) School of Alcohol Studies, which was founded in the early 1940s and gave many of the specialists in alcohol education their first training in this field.

It is partly due to all these activities, as well as to gains in the scientific approach to alcohol problems, that textbooks used for instruction about alcohol no longer show the bias noted by Roe in 1943 and that pamphlets, manuals, and other materials for teachers prepared by State Departments of Education or State Alcohol Programs are usually models of objectivity.

The view that young people should be given "the facts" and then left free to make up their own minds has prevailed for some time. But what *are* the facts, and which should have priority? Everybody agrees that it is a good thing to offer young people who are likely to begin drinking soon—or who are drinking already—some well-established facts about the physiological and psychological effects of varying amounts of alcohol. But if the main object of alcohol education is to prevent alcoholism and other forms of problem drinking, and if the teacher does not wish to exhibit a bias in favor of abstinence or of drinking, how should he proceed? To present the facts about *alcoholism* is more complicated than at first appears: honesty requires the revelation that relatively few of the people who drink, even of those who drink regularly, develop drinking problems; that no inborn physiological characteristics that render some people prone to alcoholism have been discovered; and that, even if such characteristics were known, it would be extremely difficult to imagine how they alone could cause alcoholism. Should it be explained to young people, then, that according to the modern view alcoholism results from a complex interplay of physiological, psychological, and social processes, and should they then be offered a few of the theories that have been put forward to explain this still largely obscure condition?

Alcohol educators, in facing this dilemma, increasingly accent the facts about *drinking*—that is, drinking as a form of social behavior—without neglecting what is known about the effects of alcohol. They point out that if young people are to make up their own minds about whether or not to drink, they need to know about motives for drinking, about patterns of drinking, and about the social pressures toward drinking and toward abstaining. Some educators think that high school students should know of the controversies about alcohol in our society and about the sources of our conflicting views.

Among educators who are concerned not only with what young people know but with what they do, there is increasing dissatisfaction with just teaching "the facts," for knowledge of facts by itself is not a major determinant of behavior. Such educators pay attention to evidence that whether or not a person becomes a problem drinker depends to some extent upon the way in which he is introduced to alcohol, the meaning he attaches to drinking, and the pattern of drinking that he develops. These phenomena, in turn, depend on attitudes and values, as well as beliefs and knowledge and the circumstances of the young person's life. Alcohol educators who take this view of the matter see that their task necessarily involves them in the attitude-forming processes of the young. They recognize that what young people learn about drinking, and what they do about it, may depend less on what the teacher says than on how he says it, less on what the teacher does than on what parents, other adults, and particularly other young people do. The teacher who hopes to reach the students must have a good idea of what they already know and what their preconceptions and biases are. Realizing that he cannot be neutral about patterns of drinking that he believes to be problem causing, he may nevertheless encourage good decision making on the part of his students by admitting the possibility of bias in himself, listening to opposing views, and sticking to the rules of evidence.

In general, the trend in alcohol education seems to be toward greater objectivity, more concern with drinking (rather than merely with the effects of alcohol in the body), and greater attention to the psychological and social factors that influence this kind of behavior. In most schools, however, very little time is spent on alcohol education: according to Russell (1961), current texts in the field of health devote no more than 2.5 per cent of their space to alcohol topics. This, not surprisingly, is far less than in 1910, when there was much interest in teaching the "bad effects." Alcohol problems, of course, have to compete for attention in a health-conscious nation with a wide range of other health problems. It would be a fair guess that smoking receives far more attention in the schools today than does drinking: not only is smoking the less controversial topic but, for the time being at least, the dangers of smoking seem to have captured the imagination of large segments of the public. In proportion to the amount of attention given to "problems" in general— "problems of democracy," "contemporary problems," and so forth —the amount given to alcohol is small, and in proportion to the total school curriculum it is microscopic.

One difficulty is that teachers by and large are poorly prepared to teach about alcohol and drinking. A Michigan survey of 2,736 teachers in 1964 showed that the teachers who were giving some instruction about alcohol actually knew less about the subject than the teachers who were not (Clay, 1964). The author of the survey concluded that those giving instruction were mainly abstainers, who had little except their own biases to offer the students. State programs for training teachers for alcohol education are just getting started. Professionals who might teach the teachers are few in number. Alcohol educators, though vigorous and articulate, constitute a small band.

Who is interested in alcohol education? Temperance organizations, individual citizens who have known alcoholism at first hand (in themselves or in close friends or relatives), the voluntary and governmental organizations and agencies mentioned above —but not educators in general. School people, if left alone, would probably give even less attention to alcohol education than they do now. The requirement that the facts about alcohol be taught in the schools was imposed from above, and educators know very well that the legal codes do not represent a consensus in society. Passed in the aftermath of Prohibition, the laws remain on the books because nobody lobbies for their repeal. State legislators consider that the laws probably do no harm, and they do not wish to antagonize the temperance people among their constituents. The public schools have had much experience with various groups who urge that their favorite subject be taught in the schools and who from time to time have had their way with state legislatures or local school boards. The advocates of education about driving, about sex, and about communism have had some successes in recent years, but the characteristic response to these pressures is the same as that made to the alcohol educators: it is very difficult to fit the subject into an already overcrowded curriculum. Consequently, many schools do no more than is necessary to fulfill the letter of the law.

Differences among the schools in their handling of alcohol education are due to differences not only in enlightenment about alcohol problems but in educational philosophy. In most schools, probably, education is seen as the transmission of the knowledge of the past and the teaching of the skills of communication and computation. The choice of what to teach is determined by what is taught at the next higher level of education—secondary school, college, graduate school. Such schools resist so-called "functional" courses such as health education or courses on contemporary problems and meet the requirements of alcohol education by having some of the facts about alcohol presented in a science course. Other schools, while admitting the importance of basic skills and knowledge of the past, consider that they have a responsibility to help students relate what they learn in school to their own problems and the problems of the world they are about to enter. Such schools will give alcohol education as much time as they believe they can, probably in heatlh courses. Still other schools see the major aim of education as the development of the individual's potentialities, which may be attempted either through the use of the traditional "hard" subjects or through confronting the student with contemporary problems. Schools in which this view prevails are probably most open to advanced ideas about alcohol education.

Even in these latter schools, however, alcohol education will be improved not by outside pressures such as state directives or government money for teacher training, but by a demonstration that alcohol education can be instrumental or at least parallel to the purposes the schools already have.

One basis for the schools' resistance to outside pressures is the controversial nature of most of the subjects urged by groups of citizens or professionals. Educators, by and large, do not like controversy. It upsets their routines and threatens their professional standards. The teacher who would discuss alcohol and drinking, like the teacher who has responsibility for sex or communism, is faced

with students of many backgrounds, who bring a variety of problems
and belief systems to school with them. If he confronts the issues, he
is bound to make some parents unhappy and will probably receive
suggestions from the principal that he not rock the boat; but if he
stays on safe ground, the students are likely to be bored.

Since the schools exist in society and are bound to express its prevailing value orientation, the development of enlightened
programs of alcohol education depends heavily upon the achievement of greater consensus about alcohol and drinking in the larger
society. We need to bring the whole subject into the open, to expose
the sources of our cultural ambivalence, and to work toward the development of an ethic of drinking that can reduce conflict in society
and serve as a basis for the socialization of youth.

In revising public policy with respect to drinking, we
need to know which patterns of drinking or abstaining favor the
attainment of long-range social or individual goals and which do
not. Most studies of group and personal practices, however, have not
gone far enough: their analytic categories have seldom been as
sensitive and subtle as necessary. Among the most common of these
categories is drinking versus abstaining. As a variable in research, it
has led to no guidelines that respect the full complexity of what
drinking means to self or society. The same is true of the categories
of frequency and amount, and of preference for various types of
beverages.

What is needed, as a guide both to further research and
to action, is a typology that relates each pattern of drinking and abstaining to the purposes, functioning, and development of the individual and the group. The following typology differs in two ways
from those presented in the literature: first, for reasons just given,
the present tentative scheme is frankly normative, while almost all
other typologies have aimed at value-free description; and second,
we use the same general theory in dealing with practices of both
group and individual. Each is regarded as a system and viewed in a
developmental perspective. This approach owes most to Fallding
(1964), whose typology could be used for our present purposes if it
were less complex and were applicable to the individual as well as
to the group.

Group Practices. By attending to the relations of a drinking practice to a group's purposes, functioning, and development, we may distinguish escapist, facilitative, and integrative drinking.

In a social group, *escapist drinking* would be a shared way of trying to get away from shared unpleasantness or frustration. Examples would be drinking to relieve boredom or emptiness, to get away from too much authority or restriction, to overcome anxiety or inadequacy or inferiority, or to get away from other kinds of harsh reality (such as the sense of being "trapped" in a system of work or social relations).

Such drinking is induced by problems, but it is rarely an effective means of coping with them, and it tends to create new problems of its own. Relief is likely to be temporary, and adequate coping measures are likely to be forestalled. Escapist drinking tends quickly to become "overdrinking" or even compulsive drinking. It is adopted as a way of relieving a situation, but relief does not come; hence more drinking, which attains an autonomy of its own.

In contrast, the purpose of *facilitative drinking* is to help thaw the reserve in a social group and to induce conviviality: it increases the intensity of communication, favors the free flow of information, and helps people to get acquainted. In complicated social structures, such as a business organization or a hospital, it can be an aid to communication among people of different statuses and thus make the system function more smoothly. These considerations would seem to hold in a general way for the American institution of the cocktail party, which seems to be spreading abroad. Perhaps it also holds for the common patterns of drinks before dinner, at luncheon parties, at office parties, and on other social occasions.

It would take close analysis of a given case to tell whether the drinking was really facilitating social purposes. The success of a party might depend less on facilitative drinking than on the prior friendship or congeniality of the group, in which case the drinking would border on the integrative. On the other hand, the behavior of many individuals in such situations might be determined primarily by pressures to conform, which could introduce a large element of what we are calling "escapist drinking."

The essential idea of *integrative drinking* is "all-of-a piece-with." In this case, the drinking has a meaningful place within a larger process contributing something to the achievement of its purposes, but without being essential to its existence. As Fallding (1964) points out, such drinking is a product of surplus, an adornment that can add meaning and dignity to life within a culture. As in ceremonial drinking, it might symbolize pre-existing community and thus contribute to the forging of greater solidarity, but it would not be relied upon to create community where none existed before. So also for friendship groups and families, in which relationships might be celebrated and deepened but would hardly be created by the drinking ritual.

Integrative drinking is "called for"—a phrase that has been embraced and exploited by liquor advertisers, and almost run into the ground. Not everything calls for a drink: what does is a matter of educated judgment. Drinking wine with meals would be integrative if attention were indeed given to the place of the beverage in the over-all setting, to aesthetic values, and knowledgeability. In amount, however, integrative drinking is not necessarily moderate, and may even be done with a view to becoming intoxicated provided the time and place and setting are appropriate. In the ideal case, integrative drinking would be accomplished by tolerance for the abstainer, since the drinking is not fundamentally necessary. Ideally, also, integrative drinking would be widely inclusive with respect to membership in the drinking group.

Abstaining should be looked at in the same way as drinking, with attention to its context and meaning. In some cases, abstaining is an integral part of a system of beliefs and ways, which abstaining favors and by which it is sustained. One example would be a society into which alcohol was introduced late and was then rejected on the basis that it threatened too many cherished values, a society whose leaders were able to maintain the idea of abstinence and to win wide consensus for it. In maintaining prohibition throughout their society for many years, the Hopi Indians were deliberately expressing their objection to the White Man's ways and forging solidarity within the community.

Abstinence in a social group begins to take on the aspect

of escapism, however, when the belief system of that group is threatened by all kinds of contrary beliefs in surrounding or encroaching groups, so that it becomes necessary for the group to insist rigidly upon adherence to the letter of all of its laws and to express hostility toward all surrounding groups whose ways are different.

Individual Patterns. Like the groups already discussed, individuals can be regarded as systems with purposes, functions, and patterns of development. Individuals, too, can be said to drink in escapist, facilitative, or integrative ways that relate, in this sense, to the whole personality and its manifold needs. In order for us to understand the meaning of these different types of drinking in the context of personality, it is necessary to introduce here a conception of personality and an approach to its analysis; and in order for us to see how drinking by young people can become integrated with the personality, or how escapist drinking might be avoided, we must have at hand some general principles of personality growth and development.

There are common-sense as well as technical uses of the term "personality." It is common sense to observe a person over time, to note that he is consistently aggressive or dominant or submissive, and to think of personality as the aggregate of *traits* such as these. It is also common sense to think of personality as what is referred to when a person uses the pronoun "I." The reference here is to the *self,* an aggregate of feelings, ideas, intentions, and evaluations that identifies a person to himself and distinguishes him from other people. The sense of self has continuity over time and permits one to feel that he is the same person today that he was yesterday and, with a little bit of luck, will be tomorrow.

Both of these conceptions have much in common with, but neither is the same thing as, personality as it is defined by most specialists in the field. Not all consistency of behavior can be ascribed to personality. The characteristic aggressiveness of a person, for example, may be due not so much to a persisting disposition of personality as to the fact that the person is constantly in a situation so frustrating as to evoke aggressive behavior in anyone. Personality, in its most widely accepted technical sense, refers to *dispositions* in the person that help to determine behavior and that differ from one person to another. Again, there may be durable dispositions in a person that determine some of his behavior but do not enter into his awareness, either because he is unwilling to admit their existence or because he is unable to formulate them for himself.

Personality, then, refers not to observable behavior itself but to dispositions that lie behind behavior. Observed consistencies in overt behavior and individuals' reports about themselves are important bases for inferences about personality, but the study of personality requires that these sources of information be supplemented by special techniques. In the view of most students of the subject, the dispositions of personality constitute an organized totality, a more or less enduring structure that interacts with an environment.

What are the dispositions of personality, and how are they organized? One approach to these questions—an approach that has proved useful in the past and can serve our present purpose—is to conceive of the personality as comprising three major systems: a system of primitive impulses and feelings, a system of inhibiting or punishing forces that have been automatically taken over from the social environment (the primitive conscience), and a system that controls and adapts and integrates in accord with the demands of reality (the ego). The inner life of the person consists largely in conflicts and alliances among these systems; and it is to patterns of their interaction that we may largely attribute observable traits of personality. Impulses are likely to be in conflict with the demands of conscience, the internal moral authority; and the ego has the special task of finding for impulses certain modes of gratification that are acceptable to conscience and in keeping with the requirements of reality. Anxiety, doubt, guilt, or behavior that is restricted or peculiar attends the ego's failures; satisfaction and joy attend its success.

As stated in Chapter 6, growth of the personality may be defined simply as expansion, the addition of parts and the enlargement of various parts, while development refers both to the *differentiation* of various subsystems that take on particular functions and to the *integration* of these subsystems into larger wholes. The principles of growth and development that hold for childhood hold also for the adolescent years and afterward. Adolescents and adults, as well as children, will change when confronted with stimuli that upset their equilibrium, causing instability that existing modes of adaptation do not suffice to correct. The challenges that induce growth and development are of an optimum intensity: enough to require new modes of adaptation but not so much as to lead to a falling back upon primitive, defensive stratagems.

Using the terms introduced above to stand for the major systems of the personality, one may say that a highly developed person enjoys a rich and varied impulse life, many different impulses having now found various modes of expression; that his conscience is sensitive to many different kinds of moral issues, and, having been brought under the sway of the ego, operates in accord with the person's best thought and judgment; and that his ego has at its disposal the means for judging events and controlling actions in accord with reality while knowing how to express impulses in many culturally sanctioned ways.

Against this background, we may now examine types of drinking by individuals, starting again with *escapist drinking,* the kind typically done to avoid the pains of frustration, anxiety, or emotional stress, and to gain by a short cut the gratification of impulses that cannot be admitted into the conscious ego. The problems which cause pain are real, and the relief found in drinking is genuine. The trouble is that the relief can be only temporary, and the drinking contributes nothing to the solution of the problem; indeed, it usually stands in the way of what might be effective means for coping.

A drinking pattern can be classified as escapist on the basis of its relations to personality processes without a medical diagnosis or attention to the future course of the drinking. For example, if we know that a fraternity boy drinks heavily in order to overcome doubts about his masculinity, we call that drinking escapist even though its manifest pattern does not differ from the norm for his house and even though we have reason to believe the pattern will change as he gains greater security in his male identity. With individuals as with social groups, the use of alcohol as a means for escaping temporary tensions may not be the least adaptive stratagem that could be found, nor does their use of this stratagem necessarily set in motion irreversible processes.

In the case just cited, the drinking is used as an escape from the anxiety occasioned by an unconscious conflict. In our culture drinking often symbolizes something "bad," either because the individual has connected it with repressed impulses or because he has been brought up to believe it is bad in and of itself. A common defense is deliberately to isolate drinking from the self or otherwise to render it meaningless, as in American movies, where drinking often is made to appear as casual as lighting a cigarette and is not supposed to have any effects one way or the other. A similar evasion occurs in the American youth culture when an effort is made to take the guilt away from sexual intercourse by making it just a fun thing to do.

Also classed as escapist is pure impulse expression, where an impulse has not found a channel for expression through the conscious ego. Masturbation and solitary drunkenness (which may be an unconscious equivalent of masturbation and comes under the same general ban) are of this order. There is no denying the pleasure of these acts, but there is also no denying that the pleasure is incomplete and commonly associated with disappointment—implicit recognition of the fact that these acts are poor substitutes for a larger experience that is more or less consciously imagined while they are being performed. This does not mean that we are taking a rigid position against solitary drinking, or against masturbation. As we have said, circumstances alter cases: we could not evaluate such actions without knowing their context. Certainly they are capable of being integrated in the conscious ego.

Another shortcoming of pure impulse pleasure is that when allowed full sway it is likely to lead to a focus, if not full dependence, upon a single source of pleasure—a focus that prevents the individual from cultivating other sources of pleasure through education and self-development. One might argue that pleasure is pleasure and that the repetition of a single sort of experience can be the equivalent of a wide variety of experiences. The wise hedonist would probably elect, nevertheless, to develop a variety of sources of pleasure, against the day when a source upon which he had grown dependent was cut off. He would wish to be the acquaintance of many pleasures, but the slave of none.

Facilitative drinking is widely acclaimed in our society as a means of overcoming shyness, getting courage to face a difficult situation, achieving a change of mood, relaxing after a period of stress, and producing various other desired effects in the individual. Often what is involved here is rationalization of escapist drinking; but it does appear that in some situations drinking may genuinely facilitate nondestructive purposes of the individual without impeding integration of the personality. Certainly there are shy people who find that drinking helps them to get into communication with other people, to make friends, to gain or maintain a place in the community. Initially, this is facilitative drinking; often, however, it involves some movement either toward escapist drinking or toward the integration of the drinking in the personality. If there is evidence that the activities and outcomes facilitated are increasingly capable of becoming autonomous, so that the individual is being freed of the necessity of drinking, then there is movement toward integration. If, on the other hand, no signs of such change are to be observed, it may be that the real source of the shyness is being further obscured and cut off from the rest of the personality and, hence, that drinking becomes increasingly disintegrative or escapist. Similarly with drinking to build up courage: the facilitative drinking would be moving toward integration if it enabled the individual to take a new role in a social situation, setting in motion processes that tend to change his self-conception so that on the next occasion less drinking than before was necessary in order to prepare for the test. Signs of increasing dependence on alcohol, on the other hand, would be enough to indicate that the drinking was moving toward the escapist.

Nevertheless, facilitative drinking could include some dependence on alcohol as an aid to the achievement of certain particular states, as long as the use of alcohol did not tend to increase and as long as the state of activity prepared for by drinking was not itself necessary to the maintenance of personality. For example, a woman might resort to drinking moderately every time she gave a dinner party at which strangers were to be present, without a need thus to fortify herself for any other occasions or without any change in the frequency with which these occasional parties occurred.

Drinking might be called facilitative when it helps the individual to achieve relaxation or comfort after a period of relative stress or overstimulation, and thus prepares him for a return to demanding activity. Such drinking is certainly not always integrative; nor could we call it escapist if it did not impair the individual's ability to meet the appropriate demands that were made upon him.

Integrative drinking has a place among ongoing personality processes and is thereby rendered more satisfying even as it favors the attainment of the person's larger purposes. It is not a necessity, does not interfere seriously with the satisfaction of other needs, has a place in the conscious self, is not engaged in automatically or against the will, and is not followed by regret.

The essential object of individual drinking is pleasure. When this involves reduction of inhibition and some release of impulses, which it does when satisfaction is great (as prohibitionists have always claimed), the individual is confronted with a problem of *control,* as he is whenever the gratification of basic impulses is in question. The only reliable control is that maintained by the conscious ego. Control by fear of punishment at the hands of external or internal agencies is undependable at best, and, at worst, it involves the danger of rebellious outbreaks. Control by the conscious ego means giving due attention to the demands of other needs and of reality; it means capacity to delay gratification and to govern intake in such a way as to maximize pleasure and minimize pain.

The word "control" usually suggests the restraint of behavior that might lead to trouble or cause pain, but ego control in a complex and highly integrated personality is also the means whereby the individual can maximize his pleasure. As with the indulgence of the senses generally, the deepest and most durable satisfaction from drinking comes when it is integrated with the expression of other needs, as in friendship and conviviality, or as in the connoisseur syndrome, where a whole complex of sensations and cognitions is evoked. Where drinking is integrated with other needs in the conscious ego, the individual may throw himself into the act and thus find deep satisfaction just because a variety of needs are being expressed together. Ego development is here of crucial importance: the individual cannot link his drinking with other needs until these needs are developed and find a place in the conscious ego, nor can the ego abandon itself to pleasure until it possesses enough flexibility to give assurance that it could return to its usual sober state.

In the individual, *abstaining* is integrative when that individual belongs to an abstaining culture or subculture and has decided, after deliberation, that he prefers to maintain this particular tenet of the belief system out of loyalty to the group or out of the feeling that abstaining is integral to the belief system that he wishes to support. Abstaining might be facilitative of some particular purpose of the individual, as in an athlete who believes that drinking will prevent his performing at his best. Abstaining begins to take on the features of escapism when it expresses for the individual one side of a deep-seated conflict. He might unconsciously wish to drink because drinking symbolizes for him impulses that are ordinarily forbidden expression and must be restrained at all costs. In these circumstances the individual must struggle to avoid even the thought of drinking, and he may thus be tempted to see to it that no one else drinks either. It is clear that we cannot take a position with respect to abstaining per se: here, as with drinking, our basic concern is integration, both in the social group and in the individual personality.

The Individual and the Social Group. The type of drinking that prevails in a group is associated, in general, with the same type of drinking in its individual members. If a group's drinking is integrative, for example, individuals who belong to or grow up in that group will be helped to integrate their drinking with their personalities. Conversely, a group's pattern will be in some degree dependent upon the meanings and functions that drinking has for its individual members. For example, Freedman and Kanzer (1966) became acquainted with a high school girls' club that was led—almost dominated—by a disturbed young woman whose heavy drinking, a way of carrying on a fight with her parents, became the model for her group.

The relations of individual and group drinking patterns

are not, however, as simple as might at first appear. The fact that we can identify and characterize group patterns, patterns that serve the purposes of the collectivity and that persist despite changes in its membership, does not mean that all the members of that group drink for the same reasons or that a shared way of drinking serves the same personality needs in all. For example, the excessive drinking by all the adult males in an isolated community (such as an Indian pueblo in the Southwest or the aggregate of people around a recently abandoned mine in British Columbia) might be understood as mainly due to economic depression and general demoralization. We should expect that many of the men had become personally demoralized, and some mentally disturbed, and that their drinking was escapist in the personality sense as well as in the group sense. But others might drink facilitatively, to maintain their standing in the group, while still others were resisting demoralization and drinking for pleasure. If good times were to return, all members of the community undoubtedly would be helped, and group drinking patterns would change in the direction of less escapism and more integration. But not all the men would change. Some might have found in drinking too easy an escape from ordinary personal problems, while some might have deep-seated personality disturbances that had given rise to their escapist drinking in the first place.

Similarly, integrative drinking in a group is not a guarantee that all of its members will integrate their drinking with their personalities. A college fraternity, under the leadership of seniors who had integrated their own drinking in their personalities, might maintain integrative group patterns, but this by itself would not in every case prevent individual members from using alcohol in an escapist way. Neither would being brought up in a wine-drinking society, whose drinking was integrative, eliminate those forms of problem drinking that are mainly due to individual psychopathology.

The impact of group practices upon individual behavior and personality development would seem to depend upon such factors as the group's complexity, isolation, and relations with other groups. In a simple, relatively isolated society, the individual is hardly separable from the group; his integration as a person is a more or less direct reflection of the integrated customs and ways of the group. But in a complex society such as ours, especially one that places high value upon individuality, each individual must integrate diverse social elements within himself, and his integration with society is something to be achieved. Since he is brought under the influence of diverse subcultural influences, and develops a diversity of motives within himself, he can be depended upon to conform to the ways of the major society only when he has accepted them on the basis of thought and judgment.

The significance for an individual of a group's drinking pattern also depends upon his developmental status at the time the group's influence is brought to bear. Consider teen-age drinking. Some of it can be described as a socially integrative response to shared experiences, an expression of the youthful group's solidarity. Just as Polynesian men at a "bush-beer party" appoint a steward to see that everybody is happy and that things do not get out of hand, so groups of teen-agers off for a "beer-bust" in the woods or hills often ensure that one or more of their members will remain sober enough for the drive home. Such drinking is not necessarily favorable to the later integration of drinking in the personality. It might, indeed, have a contrary effect: the immersion of the self in the peer group and a reliance upon its authority, to the detriment of ego development. Nevertheless, such drinking would appear to favor personality development more than forms of group escapist drinking designed to cope with such problems as insecurity of male identity or inability to communicate with adults.

Whether or not a particular experience will be integrated depends both on the degree of the ego's development and on whether the experience is understandable or unanticipated and shocking. A child whose ego is not yet well developed will have no trouble integrating with his ego the experience of sipping wine with members of his family who are drinking integratively; but if he witnesses drunkenness and riotous behavior on the part of his family or is seduced into drinking by older children in an atmosphere of surreptitious rebellion, his case will be different; he will be likely to associate drinking with tendencies that children ordinarily exclude from the ego. A teen-ager taught from childhood that drinking is a sin will need a more fully developed personality structure in order to integrate with it his own drinking experiences than will a teen-ager who believes that drinking is a normal adult activity. A college freshman who has grown up in an abstaining family or community and more or less automatically adopted abstinence as a way of life will have more trouble resisting pressures to drink than will a freshman who knows the facts about alcohol and drinking, has given the matter serious thought, and has thus begun to integrate his abstaining behavior with his developing ego.

Since alcohol, when taken in more than very moderate amounts, has the capacity to release impulses, drinking will raise for most teen-agers who experiment with it the general issue of impulse control. Efforts are often made by groups who would influence drinking practices in our society to remove drinking from the con-text of impulse expression by urging that it be "moderate," "reason-able," "responsible" and so on. What this often means is that, even though one drinks, the characteristic effects of alcohol are to be avoided, as when a child sips wine with his parents, a man eats sufficient food with his beer, or a lady takes a cocktail at a party but stops drinking before its effects are experienced. There is a place for these kinds of "dry" drinking, this use of alcohol as a beverage like any other, but most people who enjoy drinking want sometimes to be immoderate and temporarily "unreasonable." Within limits, it is probably a good thing to show young people that beverage alcohol is perfectly natural, nothing to get excited about, something (as the liquor ads say) that good consumers buy as they do everything else that is advertised. But since drinking for pleasure is essentially a matter of impulse expression, and will be experienced as such by teen-agers who drink, they need help through education in order to avoid both overly rigid self-restrictions and damaging outbreaks of what they have forbidden.

Alcohol education has the goal of preparing young people to assimilate the drinking they will experience. On the one hand, this preparation would avoid defining alcohol as something fearful or drinking as sinful, and on the other it would encourage young people to delay the beginning of impulse-expressive drinking until there is likelihood that their experiences will be pleasant rather than regrettable. Those parents who feel in their bones that fourteen is too young for drinking in groups away from home have the right instinct. When impulse-expressive drinking is begun too early, it is likely to become isolated from the personality and to take on meanings that make its later integration difficult or impossible; and the development of the personality itself may be impaired.

Not all who advocate a twenty-one-year limitation are either prohibitionist or seriously misguided. The effort to define drinking as an adult activity still has much to recommend it: satisfactions are greater, the richer the context to which they are assimilated. The question, of course, is when does adulthood begin? And how do we, a society that has smudged the boundary separating youth and age, prevent children from acting as if they were grown-up? We can at least accent the idea of *readiness*, and say with assurance that an eighteen-year-old is more ready than a fourteen-year-old. This would help parents, educators, and teen-agers who feel they should wait to make a case for waiting, without being moralistic and without arousing the fears of damage to physical health.

Readiness for what? For integration of drinking with ego. Teen-agers and college students need models to emulate, not just an ideal. They are focused on what adults do rather than on what they say, and the idea of postponement, even when it is in the interest of greater satisfaction later on, is likely to be regarded as another, perhaps more subtle, proscription. Unhappily, young people do not automatically blossom forth with personal responsibility and consistent value orientations as soon as they are given the freedom to do so. These virtues, like most others, have to be cultivated through an education guided by a theory of what young people need for their development rather than by what they say they want at particular times. Often, of course, they want to be very moral, and they look to the adult community for standards; on these occasions it would appear far better to offer them, as the ideal, the ideal of personality integration than to uphold authoritarian systems, which young people naturally favor as a ready means for controlling their impulses.

Adolescents often find identity and self-esteem through their membership in subcultures composed of their peers. Mem-

bership in an adolescent group, with its own culture, also serves as
a means for controlling impulses; the authority of the group becomes a substitute for parental authority. Adolescents who are meeting this and other needs in their peer groups often seem alienated
from adult society, hard to understand or to talk to; they appear
not to need parents or other adults at all. Of course they can do
without disapproving, contemptuous, or meddlesome adults, but
they are often in rather desperate need of somebody to talk to, not
only because they sometimes have serious problems but because
teen-agers are not very good at talking among themselves about
interesting or important matters. They suffer a great deal from boredom. An adult with ordinary sensitivity and some understanding of
how it is with them will not have much trouble opening channels of
communication.

In most colleges, however, the students are either
preached at or left to their own resources. College, however, is the
place where many students learn to drink and where those who
began earlier develop the patterns to which they will adhere for
years. These institutions reflect and do much to perpetuate the
drinking cultures of their larger communities. By remaining silent
on alcohol issues while discussing almost everything else, they take
part in the general conspiracy of silence; and by making unen-
forcible rules and then winking at their violation, they perpetuate
the hypocrisy that generally surrounds drinking in our society.

Yet colleges and universities have excellent opportunities
to offer alcohol education that can help to promote the development
of students, to prevent individuals from becoming problem drinkers,
and to reduce the frequency and seriousness of campus problems associated with excessive drinking by groups of students. We can begin
by recalling that college students, in general, are still caught up in
problems of how to deal with authority, manage impulses, maintain
self-esteem, and establish a suitable identity; and that, in the normal
course of events, they rapidly become more knowledgeable and
sophisticated than high school students. One aspect of their general
development is a liberalization of attitudes toward drinking and a
gradual increase of integration in the drinking that occurs. But
those changes do not just happen inevitably as functions of increasing

age or of residence at a college; they are the results of educational experiences, some of which have been planned. Many students develop very little in college, and few develop as well as they might.

In seeking to create a suitable context for alcohol education, the college administration might begin with fresh efforts to formulate policy about drinking, and ask whether some changes in policy might not favor educational goals. At conferences set up for this purpose, facts about student drinking could be presented and evaluated, as they were, for example, at the 1965 National Conference at Lake Tahoe, sponsored by the American College Health Association. Members of that conference achieved a high degree of agreement about what needs to be done and showed determination to set things in motion on their own campuses and to promote regional conferences of the same kind. Interest of this sort on the part of the colleges and universities would be very likely to influence the high schools.

Policy-making conferences might well conclude, as did the Lake Tahoe Conference, that students should have a voice in all discussions of rules about drinking. It is not that students should have the deciding voice in the making of rules or major responsibility for their enforcement. The important thing is that students be heard from, that their point of view be appreciated, and that they understand, even if they cannot fully accept, the reasons for the rules.

For many college educators, being honest with students about alcohol will reveal discrepancies between their own value positions and those expressed in state laws governing alcohol and youth. Such a revelation raises the question of what citizens can and should do about bad laws. Here the presidents and governing boards of colleges, as well as faculty members acting as individuals, can make a major contribution to the education of their students and render a substantial service to society, by taking some leadership in efforts to repeal or change such laws as the legal-age limitation, laws affecting the college campuses and the areas around them, and those that specify what is to be taught in the schools. This would be a big step toward creating that academic community that many educators now talk about so wistfully and so ineffectually.

In taking this kind of action, college educators would also have to see to it that the drinking on their campuses was increasingly integrative and that the views of abstainers were respected. If the legal-age limitation were removed, or lowered to eighteen, the colleges would be free to make their own rules about drinking, an opportunity requiring full attention to the drinking practices and attitudes that prevail on each particular campus. Suddenly to permit drinking on a campus where most of the students do not drink, and where those who do carry on in a spirit of rebellion or male cultism, will be asking for trouble. On another campus the same change of rules would merely legitimize current practices.

Colleges that wish to make the drinking of their students more integrative will want to consider the establishment of campus drinking places, and the better utilization of those that already exist. Experience suggests that campus pubs or rathskellers encourage moderation and help the students to place drinking in a context of integrative experiences; whereas the common patterns of off-campus drinking tend to be immoderate or even destructive, and highly unfavorable to the integration of drinking in the personality. At the same time, campus drinking places that are visited by faculty members as well as by students can provide students with models of integrative drinking and perhaps, through encouraging informal encounters, lead to some improvement in faculty-student relations. This is not to suggest, however, that drinking together on the part of faculty and students, whether in a public place or in the faculty member's home, is generally desirable: it depends on the kinds of relationships that already exist, and the kinds that are to be encouraged. Drinking together implies intimacy and the absence of status boundaries—things which both faculty and students usually prefer to approach with caution. On the other hand, faculty and students do sometimes become friends; and if this were celebrated by means of a drink, the act would be integrative. Drinking together to mark the student's surmounting of academic hurdles or his admission to a community of scholars would also be integrative.

Alcohol education can occur not only in the classroom or in a social setting but as a part of research. For example, students might be interviewed as subjects in a study and then offered feedback in discussion groups. With older students, tests could be offered to determine susceptibilities to problem drinking, and followed by counseling sessions. This procedure for embedding an educational program in a program of research would not only reduce students' resistance to learning about alcohol but arouse their interest and curiosity. Instead of merely telling students "what they ought to know," researchers would invite them to help in an attack on some very difficult scientific questions. In talking with them about the results, researchers would assume that everyone is interested in scientific findings and would capitalize on the fact that students, like everyone else, are interested in themselves and their functioning. Most of what was said to them, far from being in the form of a lecture, would be in response to questions. Taking part in an experiment would by itself have favorable effects upon students; they would be offered the experience, rare for them, of contact with adults who see them out of interest alone.

In addition, such a program would probably reduce the number of alcohol-related disciplinary problems brought to the attention of the dean, as well as the number of alcohol-related injuries treated at the Student Health Service. Students who were tested and counseled would tell their friends and acquaintances about their experience; the research team would probably be called upon to explain its work to various campus groups; and discussion of alcohol and drinking would move to a higher level of awareness and sophistication than before.

Students can take part in inquiries not only as subjects but as junior members of research teams or even as independent investigators working under supervision. In addition to collecting data on attitudes and practices on their own campuses, they could go into the field as part of courses in social science or psychology, getting to know some men on skid row or looking into what goes on in treatment centers for alcoholics. If some students learn, in depth, about alcohol problems, they can be counted upon to inform others. In a course, for example, they can be given the opportunity to lead a section or make reports. No one doubts that much of what students learn, particularly what is immediately relevant to their social lives in school and afterward, they learn from each other. Since aspects of this learning that are most valuable to students could easily be spoiled by adult intervention, efforts by school administrations to induce "reliable," adult-oriented students to do their work for them should be discouraged: such students are often authoritarian and, even when given formal leadership roles, lack the confidence of their fellows. On the other hand, genuine student leaders do sometimes seek from adults—those in whom *they* have confidence—knowledge and advice to use in their work with other students. For example, the leaders of a fraternity may be at a loss when it comes to "educating" their pledges; or the older students involved in student-run "big brother or big sister" programs may welcome some adult guidance. These are excellent opportunities for spreading knowledge and encouraging mature attitudes about alcohol and drinking as about other campus issues.

Opportunities for weaving material about alcohol and drinking into regular courses are greater in college than in high school, not only in biology, history, and literature but in the newer social sciences. In addition, colleges offer facts and principles from those disciplines which, in addition to biology, we rely upon for explanations of alcohol-related phenomena—from sociology, anthropology, political science, and psychology, as well as from pre-professional courses that begin to prepare for careers in such fields as social welfare, education, public health, and criminology. In all of these disciplines alcohol-related phenomena can be used to illustrate general principles and to confront students with unsolved scientific and practical problems. The intellectual grasp of the subject which the student obtains in this way can serve him in his daily life as well as in his future roles of researcher, professional, or opinion-leader.

12

The Integration of Sexuality in the Personality

A few years ago the president of one of this country's leading women's colleges attracted national attention with a speech in which she called on the young women in her charge to maintain high standards of sexual morality. The very fact that such a speech was made somehow suggested to the public that the young women in this college must be preoccupied with sex and were probably engaging in all sorts of riotous sexual behavior, which needed to be cracked down on. At about the same time, the student health service at another leading university was pegging its argument not on virtue but on discretion. One must be very careful, students there were told, because of the dangers of pregnancy and other inconveniences that might result from any liberated sexual behavior. And simultaneously both men and women students were, as usual, being exposed to an enormous popular literature —*Playboy* magazine, Brown's *Sex and the Single Girl,* Greene's *Sex on the Campus*—which, far from discouraging sexual freedom on any grounds, seemed to take it for granted that "everybody's doing it." Such are the contradictory messages beamed toward the young.

This whole state of

affairs left me with the impression that young people today face an extremely difficult task in trying to find a defensible position on the matter of sexual behavior. Adults are saying little to help them. If we, as educators, hope to offer any kind of meaningful guidance, we had better have an understanding of the place of sex in personality functioning. In the present chapter, therefore, I want to discuss certain theoretical issues regarding the integration of sexuality in personality and then to suggest the possibility of working out a sexual morality, or ethic, that is suitable for our times.

The question of what the youth are up to is always an intriguing one for adults, and since actual knowledge is hard to come by, fantasies are readily stimulated by popular literature and the daily press. For example, the old game of trying to estimate how many college women are virgins has been made somewhat more exciting by the advent of college psychiatry and the local birth-control clinics, to say nothing of studies such as the Kinsey report. But a large proportion of the students seen by college psychiatrists and at planned-parenthood clinics are those who act out their problems through unconventional sexual behavior. Although a minority, these students are likely to know, and to tell their psychiatrists about, other students who are doing the same thing; further, they participate in the natural tendency for those who deviate to overestimate the number of their peers who are similarly inclined. Thus, professional people are easily led to overestimate the amount of uninhibited sexuality that exists on our campuses. And, aware of readers' lively interest in the behavior of our huge population of college students, popular writers have not missed the opportunity to make something sensational out of the professional reports.

Although it is difficult to get reliable details about the sexual behavior of college students, my colleagues and I have been studying student behavior in general during the past twelve years at an Eastern women's college, a Western state university, and a Western private university. In the course of these studies, we interviewed representative samples of undergraduate populations several times a year during their four college years, establishing relationships of mutual confidence and learning some facts about these students' sexual behavior (Freedman, 1964; Katz *et al.*, 1966; Sanford,

1966). We cannot, of course, generalize from these populations to all college students, but, since the institutions at which we have worked are among the least conventional in the land, I have no hesitation in saying that there is no general decline in student morality.

If we look, for example, at rates of premarital intercourse, we find that about 25 to 35 per cent of the women in our samples were not virgins, in the technical sense of the term, at the time of graduation; in the Western institutions where we have worked, the rate for young men was approximately 50 per cent.* The general picture is not radically different from that offered by Kinsey and his co-workers (Kinsey and Gebhard, 1953), who interviewed large samples of students and adults in the 1930s and formed the opinion that there had been no great change since the 1920s. Furthermore, most of the women who engage in premarital sex relations are either engaged to be married or else involved in serious relationships that they believe will be durable. Most college women, however, probably a higher proportion than thirty years ago, do engage in some form of sexual experimentation, such as necking and petting.

On the other hand, although rates of premarital intercourse may or may not have changed radically since the 1920s, it seems that the circumstances and meaning of this behavior *have* changed. In the 1920s and 1930s college women who engaged in

* When published elsewhere, our figures on rates have been greeted with some disbelief. Students and worried mothers have written to say that, according to their observations, rates are much higher. I would suggest that in this matter our eyes may easily deceive us. Looking with amazement at the hundreds of exhibitionist or deliberately provocative young people "along the Avenue" or "around the Square" (not all of whom are students), we forget about the thousands of quietly conventional people in the high-rise dorms who are also shocked by the "goings-on." Let us bear in mind also that a dangerously large—and apparently growing—number of our citizens are willing to believe anything about students, who, as a new "outgroup," are becoming the heirs of the negative imagery that used to be projected onto Jews and Communists. There is great need for a national survey of student sexual behavior and attitudes—one as carefully done as were our interviews with small samples of students. Until the results of such a survey are available, thoughtful citizens who cannot accept our findings or conclusions should at least withhold judgment; for otherwise they might easily lend support to a new form of authoritarian thinking.

premarital intercourse may have been submissive, somewhat maso-chistic persons who could be seduced because they felt that they had little else to offer. But today, at least in the colleges that my col-leagues and I have observed, girls who engage in sexual intercourse do so with their eyes open, with quite a bit of soul-searching, and usually, as I have said, when they are involved in a serious relation-ship. And there is, of course, a great deal more awareness and frank discussion of sexual matters today than there was thirty years ago. Surely a higher proportion of college students are including sexuality in their conscious schemes of things. They try to make their sexual behavior an integrated part of themselves and of a genuine love relationship. But they are finding it increasingly difficult to accept either nineteenth-century morality or the pragmatic advice to "be-careful" as the basis for a sound sexual ethic, which is something most of them would like to develop.

All societies have arrangements—law, custom, taboo, or religious ritual—for controlling or regulating sexual behavior in order to ensure peace among individuals and to stabilize relation-ships that are necessary for the care of children. In the United States we have relied mainly upon the Judaeo-Christian ethic, both in its ideal of the fully developed and humanized personality and in its Puritanical version. But the latter seems to have persisted, often taking the form of total rejection of pleasure, so that wide gaps have arisen between what was professed and what was practiced.

With World War I came radical changes in behavior, including increases in rates of premarital intercourse and, of course, in other forms of sexual behavior. Efforts to find moral or phil-osophical bases for the new freedom often took the form of ideolo-gies claiming that the gratification of sexual impulses was "natural" or necessary to health, or else nothing but a form of play.

Where do we stand today? We still seem to be in a state of general confusion, and young people who have to work out suitable patterns of sexual behavior are confronted with widespread cultural ambivalence. Our culture exhibits an enormous preoccupa-tion with sex, as shown in our movies, popular literature, and ad-vertising; yet no authoritative voice questions the idea of monogamy or suggests that sex should not become a part of love. American movies, typically, seek to carry titillation as far as possible, while paying respects to conventional morality. As a result, normal sexuality is played down, and pathology of various kinds is emphasized. A youthful movie-goer, for example, could easily get the impression that sex is mainly a matter of power: that women want to be overpowered by men, and that if a man is not sadistic enough to satisfy this need he will turn into a cheerful incompetent, to be ruled by a dominant woman. Thus, the young person growing up in our society finds himself surrounded with sexual stimuli but does not learn how the mature or healthy adult should express the impulses that are aroused.

Sexual behavior has a wide range of different meanings for different people. The desire for immediate pleasure is only one of many possible motives for sexual activity. More fundamental than this may be the young person's concern with his personal identity and his relations to other people—his peers of both sexes, his parents, and other adults. For example, a young woman might permit herself to be drawn into a sexual relationship because she has a low opinion of herself and feels that she has little else to offer; she may regard sexual submission as the only means to secure the attentions of her partner or as a means for having at least a temporary sense of being wanted; or she might use her sexual behavior to express rebelliousness and a desire to punish her parents. In their heterosexual activity, young men may express a need to assure themselves of their adequacy as males or to demonstrate for others their power or superiority. Much sex activity of young men is fundamentally homosexual in its meaning, for they want status and solidarity within the male peer group and may seek it through conquests and boasting.

Young people of both sexes may find in sexual activity a source of thrills, a sense of being fully alive and "in communication"—the same sort of thing that some try to enhance through drugs. Or they may belong to a group that accepts one of the contemporary ideologies according to which sex is essentially meaningless, just "a fun thing" to do or a "natural impulse," any inhibition of which is "neurotic."

Clearly these kinds of sexual behavior differ from those in which the partners know and respect each other and themselves, and are sensitive to each other's feelings, and in which sex is part of a durable relationship based upon love. In this light it seems a serious mistake to follow Kinsey, the zoologist, in regarding the study of sexual behavior as a matter of counting "outlets" (Kinsey, Pomeroy, and Martin, 1951), as if all "outlets" were equal, psychologically and morally.

Abstaining from sexual activity should also be regarded in a differentiated way. It is one thing to refrain merely because of fear of punishment, or fear of closeness to people, or from anxiety over the expression of feeling; it is something else to hold back because one is not ready or prefers to await the development of a clearer sense of identity or believes that sex belongs to a relationship based on love.

How are we able to evaluate or understand such diverse behavior patterns, considering their many meanings and effects? Puritanism, pragmatism, the "Playboy" ethic, and other existing ideologies hardly seem adequate to do the job. Some new standard is needed, one that reflects our growing understanding of man and human society. I propose that we can find this standard in the concept of *integration;* that here, as in the case of drinking, we should place higher value upon behavior patterns that favor integration both in the personality and at the social level.

We may speak of integration in the personality when the sexual behavior takes its place among other needs in the conscious ego, the individual now finding deep satisfaction because a variety of needs are being expressed together. Far from interfering with the person's functioning in other areas, sexual activity would now provide a channel for the expression of a great variety of feelings and dispositions, and it would, at the same time, become more meaningful because it was closely tied up with other satisfactions. At the social level, integration is achieved in a relationship between two people—one that is rendered the more meaningful and durable because sex is a part of it and one in which sexual activity is the more satisfying because of the pre-existing social and psychological context in which it takes place.

This emphasis on relationship should not be taken to mean that lovers can forget about the rest of society and think only of each other. Their public behavior may influence that of others, and they will do well to ask themselves whether this influence might not be socially *dis*integrative—whether, for example, a display of their relationship might not encourage imitation by people far less mature than themselves. By the same token, two young people who have found a satisfactory pattern of behavior may be better off if they do not have to regard themselves as deviant. A highly integrated society can tolerate a great deal of deviance, and highly integrated individuals can, if they have to, stand against society; but a society cannot exist without some more or less acceptable standards and patterns of sexual practice. These standards and patterns will probably always be needed by ordinary citizens, and even the most highly developed autonomous individual will sometimes need external support for his values.

Let us consider how sex might be well integrated in the personality. The fundamental principle is the same as that set forth in the chapter on alcohol. In order for integration to occur, there must first be a good measure of personality development, a more or less substantial structure with which sexual experiences can be integrated; and the experiences must in themselves be assimilable— neither too shocking nor altogether unanticipated. The individual cannot relate his sexual behavior to other needs unless they have developed and found a place in the conscious ego, nor can the ego abandon itself to pleasure unless it possesses enough flexibility to give assurance that it can return to its more typical state as reality requires. When these conditions are not met, there occur those gross failures in sex adjustment that are detailed in psychiatric textbooks. Many patients, for example, were taught as children that sexual activity is sinful and likely to be followed by catastrophe; and since these patients' undeveloped egos could not cope with the conflict thus engendered, sexual impulses were repressed and followed by symptoms which could be understood either as extraordinary efforts to keep the impulses repressed, or as disguised or distorted manifestations of the impulses themselves. Sexual maladjustment is not, however, always due to the stern warnings and rigid prohibitions of parents; it may be the result of premature exposure to sexual stimuli. Sex experiences in childhood may easily be misunderstood or tied to infantile impulses or fantasies that have already been made unconscious and thus separated from the developing ego.

One college student whom we interviewed a few years ago (Sanford, 1966) provided a striking example of the hazards of precocious sexuality. This young woman was an imposing figure on the campus and a high achiever in her chosen field of art. She led an almost totally uninhibited sexual life, for which she had articulated some sophisticated philosophical ideas. She had had frequent sexual intercourse before entering college and had never really had what the psychoanalysts call a "latency period." It appeared that she had always been preoccupied with sex and as a little girl had been aroused in playing "the doctor game." One's first impression might be that this girl presented a picture of total freedom, but psychological testing and intensive interviewing revealed that she had a full gamut of ethnocentric, anti-Semitic, and authoritarian attitudes; that behind a façade of freedom and liberality were deep anxieties, expressed in nightmares; and, perhaps most seriously, that she wanted to marry a man who would dominate her, make her behave, and tell her when the party was over and it was time to go home.

Although there may be exceptions, it is not easy for a girl to be the image of sexual freedom and at the same time a fully developed person. The woman whose story is told in the bit of pornography entitled *The Housewife's Handbook on Selective Promiscuity* (Anthony, 1962) is a caricature of a free person. This character is able to get a lot of pleasure from a wide range of sexual affairs, and she is articulate enough to give some psychological interpretations of her behavior. Unfortunately, however, she is unable to maintain any stable relationships with people. She has several children by as many different men but is unable to maintain a continuing relationship with any of the latter. She is strongly narcissistic and strongly exhibitionistic, traits that are incompatible with being a fully developed personality.

Maladjustments of this kind, as well as neurotic inhibitions, have for a long time been the concern of a literature on sex education that recommends protecting children from exposure to experiences that might gratify and shock at the same time, avoiding dire warnings and stern reproaches, and, as the need becomes apparent, giving the factual information necessary to avoid serious misunderstanding. For college students such sex education seems beside the point, though they sometimes show surprising gaps in their factual information. Many of them, however, still have a long way to go developmentally before they can integrate their sexuality, personally and socially. The problem now is not to avoid further repression but to add meaning, and thus to realize the possibilities of full integration. Difficulties arise both from social pressures toward premature commitment to social roles or styles of life and from immaturity of personality.

With respect to social pressures, girls in our society today are in a rather vulnerable position. They are under pressure to define themselves narrowly in terms of sex roles, as sex objects or as potential mothers. Often they are forced into these roles in ways that make further development difficult. Sometimes they are led to self-conceptions that are hard to revise or modify. Many lower- and lower-middle-class girls find themselves in these roles because sex has been thrust upon them before they have had a chance to develop their personalities. Such are the demands of their roles that they are often lost to further education.

College women, on the other hand, are freer of such self-conceptions and role commitments, and when reasonably well-developed in their ego functioning, they find it less difficult than is commonly supposed to inhibit overt sexual behavior. Many things besides sex seem important to them, and there is now a large organization of conscious needs and purposes that has become the basis for self-respect and that can be set in opposition to any particular desire. I have elsewhere (Sanford, 1963) described in detail a young woman who as a college senior was still a virgin and expected to remain so until her marriage but who was rated high on "sexual adequacy" by the psychologists who had interviewed her from time to time throughout her four college years. In summarizing her case I wrote as follows:

Penny . . . is striving to make sexuality a part of her conscious self, and to a considerable extent she has accomplished this. She has conscious sexual fantasies of an explicit sort, is aware of the emotions that normally accompany sexual feeling, and is prepared to take responsibility for her actions. . . . One might say that she is trying to arrange things so that when she gives herself sexually it is her *self* that she gives. It is this that gives the impression of strong sexuality, for, when sex is fully integrated with the ego, it can be a channel for the expression of a rich assortment of feelings and emotions. Such integration also means, of course, that sex experiences can now become a means for the further development of the personality; like other important experiences, it can take its place within an expanding structure of integrated processes (p. 31).

Of course, the expressed desire "to wait" is not always a mark of gradual movement toward the integration of sexuality in the personality; it might, for example, be based upon neurotic inhibition. One could, however, pretty well rule out this possibility where there was, as in Penny's case, the conscious acceptance of so many aspects of sexuality, including its fearful aspects. But in sharpest contrast to Penny would be the young woman mentioned above, who could admit no fears or inhibitions having to do with sex or men but who was driven by unconscious fantasies that expressed themselves in compulsive behavior and in nightmares.

Although boys have a greater chance to escape early role commitments, they are by no means exempt from pressures toward premature definition through primitive "masculinity." If they grow up in a subculture that measures maleness in terms of sexual activities, and if they begin obtaining gratification of impulses through dehumanized sex, then it is more difficult for them to achieve the capacity to delay gratification that seems to be so essential for personality development.

Such an overaccent on male identity is often a manifestation of authoritarianism in personality. Young men who have not escaped this personality syndrome are strongly disposed to see all women either as "pure," sweet and passive or as prostitutes; and naturally they tend to marry those who seem to belong to the first class. Frequently they are disappointed, for girls who are understandingly soft and sweet on the surface often turn out to be aggressively demanding underneath. Authoritarian young women, on the other hand, characteristically marry dominant "go-getters"— who not infrequently turn out to be dependent underneath.

Authoritarianism is thus a fairly reliable mark of unreadiness for a sexual relationship. It gradually declines under the liberalizing influences of college, but college men and women are usually slow to revise their stereotypes of one another. Residential arrangements and patterns of "dating and rating" often make it difficult for students to know members of the opposite sex as individuals, and persisting sexual inequalities (such as different rules for women) serve to perpetuate the idea that the sexes are categorically different in their psychology. One can sympathize with the young man who demands more "sexual freedom" in the hope that through dehumanized sex he may demonstrate his masculinity or boost his self-esteem; but one can sympathize more with the young woman who prefers "to wait" rather than allow herself to be used for such purposes. Neither men nor women can develop fully under conditions of sexual discrimination, which reinforces authoritarianism in men and impairs the self-respect of women. For this reason, we may applaud the growing sophistication of college women, their growing insistence upon equality in their relations with men. College authorities, knowing these things, will not meet student demands for more sexual freedom merely by negotiating about specific rules; they will, instead, renew their efforts to overcome authoritarianism and to create a community in which young men and women can get to know each other, and themselves, as human beings.

A consideration of the cultural and social situation in which many of our young people live, in and outside of college, makes it clear that our "ethics of integration" is not likely to be immediately attractive or universally relevant. In an important sense we are talking here about a type of middle-class morality, which assumes that the individual has some stake in the larger society and some orientation toward the future. It can have little meaning for those who are alienated from middle-class society and who have learned to live in the present because the future appears to hold no promise. Our society shows a tendency to allow freedom of impulse to those who are not to be admitted to full membership, just as those who feel rejected by society often turn to impulse expression as a major aspect of life. If our middle-class morality is to be more useful for those who live in poverty, then there must be some social reconstruction in order to assure the poor that they too can achieve middle-class objectives.

In some important respects students are like the poor. Many of them live in states of emotional deprivation, and there is some danger of their becoming alienated from contemporary society. Often under enormous pressure from the academic apparatus, they are forced to do much work that is meaningless to them, and to make other painful sacrifices. They have to have some assurance that it is all worth the candle, and that their idealism is not completely inapplicable in the world today.

In the light of research on the general personality development of college students and on their behavior and attitudes concerning sex, there are good reasons to believe that the general approach here will prove useful to them and to those who work with them. Promiscuity or casual sexual relationships rarely, if ever, have been found to express emancipation in students; most commonly they are found to reflect pathology that is unfavorable to further development. Sexual intercourse between college students who have entered upon durable relationships sometimes is something very good, but the young people involved do not always meet their obligations to maintain personal integration and to assume social responsibility.

Most favorable to personality development, our studies suggest, is a gradual approach to sexuality, one that is accompanied by thoughtfulness, self-discovery, and increasingly differential perceptions of other people. Students who develop in this way find the control and the expression of their impulses less difficult. Perhaps the greatest immediate benefit of "ethics of integration" would be support for those students who want to delay sexual experimentation without fearing that they are neurotic, or puritanical, or unlike most other students.

Young people who want to be integrated sexually must become familiar with the emotional impulses underlying sexual behavior. This means that we may expect not only some preoccupation with and much discussion of sex but also some experimentation. And if young people are to develop their personalities, they must gradually replace external controls with internal ones. This means that we can expect them to go to great lengths to find out whether adults mean what they say and practice what they preach. If students are to accept conventional standards, they must first test the validity of these standards.

The college assumes the task of helping its students to develop their personalities. All its resources and practices, including its actions and policies with respect to sex, should be directed to this end. This kind of education must be guided by knowledge of what students experience and by a theory that recognizes individual differences at different stages of development. A problem for the college is how to offer students sufficient protection from the demands of their own impulses and the importunities of their peer culture, while at the same time encouraging development of inner controls by assuming that the students are maturing successfully. Students have to be protected and at the same time trusted, even though the trust will not be justified in all cases. This is a difficult problem, and it will continue to be a disconcerting one.

At all times, however, educators must bear in mind that the students are there to be educated and that the actions affecting them should have this aim, rather than that of pleasing the alumni or protecting the image of the college. When a student breaks a rule, his case should be handled with attention first to his educational needs. Disciplinary crises involving groups of students or taking the form of "scandals" can be, and sometimes have been, made occasions for special efforts at education in community or ethical sensitivity.

Deans simply can no longer be satisfied with roles as disciplinarians or with images of themselves as stern but fair fathers or mothers. They are going to have to learn to take some positive actions that are designed to teach personal and social integration. For example, instead of merely tolerating the usual outmoded systems of "dating and rating" and contending that occasional wild parties are natural ways of "letting off steam," they should work toward creating situations in which young men and women get to know each other as people. Above all, there should be continuous communication with students, not through lectures but through discussion in which any controversial issue may be brought into the open and any pattern of campus behavior may be exposed for analysis and criticism. Only then can college authorities and college students work together to develop valid ethical principles that are acceptable to the large majority of the educational community.

IV

The
Educational
Environment

13

The Power
of the College
Peer Culture

During the 1950s we read a great deal about the passivity, conformity, and indifference of the American college student. Some of these observations were based on the report of the Cornell Values Study (Goldsen *et al.*, 1960), which surveyed the opinions and attitudes of 2,975 students in eleven universities. The major finding of this research was that "the present generation of college students is politically disinterested, apathetic, and conservative. Social movements and social philosophies do not arouse their interests or command their commitment." Philip Jacob (1957) put it more dramatically, accusing students of being "unabashedly self-centered in outlook, aspiring above all to material gratification of themselves and their families." Gillespie and Allport (1955) and Riesman (1960) agreed that American college students of the 1950s were given to "privatism."

Nor does the situation appear to have changed much in the decade or so since the Cornell study; for although the Free Speech Movement, peace marches, freedom schools, and tutoring for the underprivileged have all attracted a good deal of attention, only a small minority of college students are actively involved (see the table in Chapter 8). Most college students of today are as passive as their brothers of the 1950s.

Passivity reflects not only a certain pedagogic reluctance in our official academic culture but also the good-natured resistance of student peer cultures. Recent studies (including Freedman, 1956; Suchman, 1958; Goldsen *et al.*, 1960; and Bushnell, 1962) leave no doubt that what students learn in college is determined in large measure by their fellow students or, more precisely, by the norms of behavior, attitudes, and values that prevail in the peer groups to which they belong. Not all students, of course, accept the prevailing, or primary, student culture, and others grow away from it in their senior year; but by definition, a majority of the students are participating more or less fully in this culture.

In ten years of developmental studies of students (Sanford, 1956, 1962), we have found that peer cultures in rather widely varying institutions have certain outstanding features in common. Students are expected to be friendly, cooperative, and pleasant toward one another, and polite, dutiful, and impersonal toward the faculty. College work is to be taken seriously, but not too seriously; frivolity is discouraged, but outstanding scholarly work is only tolerated, not applauded. In most areas of student life the accent is on moderation and leveling. If a student studies too much or dates too much, thinks too much or talks too much, is too ambitious or too indifferent, the peer culture has effective means for bringing him into line. With respect to ideas and issues, he is expected to be openminded and noncontroversial—above all, to avoid unpleasantness. If an ethical decision has to be made, the proper course is to see first what the others think.

Of the college and its policies, the peer culture is usually uncritically accepting. When unpleasant situations arise, it saves itself from involvement by saying, "Well, we're only going to be here another year or two." Similarly, the peer culture does not feel required to have opinions on affairs of the world: "We are only students, learning how to think, and there is so much to be said on both sides." As tolerant of people as of ideas, the peer culture practices little exclusion on the basis of race, religion, ethnic group, or social background: anyone can belong, so long as he does not deliberately reject the peer culture or defy its ways.

Regarding the future with optimism, the peer culture envisions a stable but highly complex society in which the reward for "fitting in" will be a happy—that is to say, a materially gratifying—life. The student is prepared to fit into this life by the friendly, cooperative, agreeable, tolerant, and optimistic tone of the peer culture. When these students err, it is usually on the side of over-realism, which often happens when people are somewhat anxious; and they are likely to sacrifice adequacy of long-run perspective for short-run practicality. In this respect they are like some of the more sheltered academicians.

In their social adaptability, students are participating in a national tradition noted by De Tocqueville and by subsequent visitors to this country. René de Roussey de Sales quoted one of his compatriots to the effect that of the three great democratic nations the British had specialized in liberty, the French in equality, and the Americans in fraternity; and European observers are still remarking on our idealization of teamwork and on the importance we attach to getting along with people. Although these values may lead to admirable cooperation, neither our sociability nor our practicality provides support for the lonely intellectual work characteristic of the academic culture.

With varying degrees of success, colleges attempt to create a "climate" reflecting the academic values of the faculty and administration. They may, for example, promote small extracurricular groups in which students participate with their professors and assimilate a common set of intellectual values. For most students, however, the most important subsociety in the college is that to which only students belong—the world of cocurricular activities, of such formal structures as student government, and of various informal friendship, living, or interest groups. In this world, the student can find support, friendship, and prestige. It may promote his development by providing an opportunity to become familiar with a variety of social roles and by confronting him with situations in which he can learn to adapt. The problem is, these roles and forms of adaptation may divert attention from, or even counteract, the academic culture.

Bushnell (1962) has suggested that the student culture and the academic (faculty and administration) culture of the typical American college are in a "contact situation," in which the faculty has accepted the task of "acculturating" the "underdeveloped nation" of students, while the students, with a fairly realistic view of the requirements for a pleasant life on the campus and of what is needed to achieve a secure life after graduation, are much taken up with socialization and "enculturation" within their own group. Bushnell describes some of the bases and forms of the students' resistance to acculturation—for example, by surface compliance or superficial adaptation while keeping the faculty at a distance and refusing to internalize their offerings, or by accepting an offering but using it for purposes not intended by the donor, as in using course content for small talk over cocktails.

On occasion, however, the two cultures are complementary rather than competitive. For example, one girl whom we interviewed as a freshman at Vassar was a serious, constricted, and rather anxious scholar in mathematics and physical science. She was closely attached to her family and had already sought and found the support of several teachers, although she was inclined to keep her distance from them. The research staff predicted she would change little in college, a prediction which was valid for three years. But when she was seen in her senior year, she seemed a different person: she dressed more casually and gayly, carried herself with greater freedom and relaxation, and displayed a wide range of interests, a set of advanced social attitudes, and openness with respect to plans for her future. It turned out that she had been rooming for two years with a group of very bright, adventurous, and warmhearted girls, who apparently had taken it upon themselves to "bring her out." It did not appear that they had destroyed her scholarly interests, but they had certainly changed her conception of the roles she might take.

Often, however, academic ambition is vitiated by the peer culture. It is not uncommon to encounter young women who arrive at college with the announced intention of preparing for professional training—in medicine, for example, or in chemistry—and who give up this intention in their first year, mainly under the impact of student society. Such a girl might come from a family of relatively low economic status, or from a small-town public high school, or from an ethnic minority, where her intellectual interests were linked with social isolation. The student society, in its tolerant, egalitarian, and socially skillful way, takes her in and shows her that she can attain what she wants—for example, status, acceptance, and a happy social life—without going to such an extreme as to study medicine or chemistry.

Most entering students, as we have observed them, seek acceptance by their fellows and are eager to assimilate the prevailing student culture. For many students this process requires virtually no adjustment, since they bring a very similar culture with them from their secondary schools; for others the process of assimilation is more or less automatic; and for still others it is a matter of some deliberate choice or effort. Only a small minority succeed in remaining aloof.

Among the many arenas of peer culture are rooming groups, such as the one described for us by a Vassar student: "I have two roommates, one of whom I knew very well at school. Two of her friends are next door. We are all very compatible. . . . We never lose our tempers with each other. We all come from more or less the same backgrounds . . . are interested in the same things and have good discussions. We just seem to like the same people, and to have the same friends: girls who don't talk about boys and clothes all the time but yet are fun." Within such a group, the girls reassure one another that they are "all right," or beyond moral reproach, and meanwhile project their feelings of badness on people outside. While providing this reassurance, however, the group also restricts the social freedom of its members; and as they unconsciously feel the need to reject and go beyond the group, the girls begin to fear obscurely that it will likewise reject them. Ordinarily they react by clinging ever more tightly to the group—an aspect of peer culture no less dismaying than its nonacademic values. The peer culture also draws support from the neurotic unwillingness of some students to hurt anyone by disagreeing with him, from the conscience-driven need to sacrifice all for the good of the group, and from the attitude that one might go along with the group because it is the easiest thing to do.

Conformity is promoted not only by social pressures but by authoritarianism in the personality. Among college students, some of the most distinctive authoritarians are sorority girls whose social group has replaced parents as the external agency of control—the agency toward which they display the same blind loyalty, mixed with suppressed hostility. I recall a young woman at Vassar who as a freshman seemed to be a free spirit, open to intellectual forces. Her freedom was premature, however; she was not so much free as impulse-ridden. For her, only the peer culture could offer the necessary structure and control. She was a good student, but the values with which she emerged at the end of her senior year were those common among her fellow students: conservatism, privatism, and practicality.

In the face of such a student culture, the college is not entirely helpless, although many pretend to be or simply ignore the problem. One approach is to try to bring the peer culture more into harmony with academic goals; and another, to free individual students from the domination of their peers.

Changing the Content of the Peer Culture. Student culture is determined not only by events in the larger society but also by the social structure of the college as a whole and by the composition of the student body; hence, it can be changed by deliberate action or, as Newcomb (1962) has shown, enlisted in the service of at least some of the faculty's educational purposes. In colleges that have been able, largely through vigorous recruitment and selection, to create a campus society in which the highest prestige attaches to the highest scholarship, the student's need to belong will help to keep academic motivation at a high level.

To change the student culture of an institution is, of course, a very difficult business, requiring perseverance. Ordinarily there seems to be a lag of at least two student generations, or about a decade, in the changing of a college's public "image" through changes in selection. Meanwhile, the change might begin with the growth of a student-faculty subculture centering, for example, on a particular experimental program or philosophical outlook. Approaches of this kind, whatever their scope, seek not to change the student's inclination toward conformity but rather to exploit it in the interest of intellectual goals.

Freeing the Student from His Peers. If, however, we are concerned with conformity itself, not the particular value systems or behavior patterns with which the individual conforms, then changing the content of the peer culture is not enough. We must to some extent free the student from the claims of *any* peer culture.

Conformity is a disposition to believe and behave as prestigeful others do, regardless of the real merit of those beliefs and behavior patterns, and regardless of the integrity of one's self. We oppose this kind of conformity not because we want people to share our opposition to particular beliefs but because we want them to develop as individuals. We want them to be aware of sources of bias within themselves, to arrive at opinions through their own thought processes, and to integrate their rational beliefs with their personalities so that their convictions can stand against the crowd. In short, we want them to become differentiated, complex, and autonomous.

Happily, the college that mobilizes its various academic resources in the interests of a liberal, developmental education for its students is already on the road toward freeing them of conformity for conformity's sake. Although some students can never be freed from conformity by methods short of intensive psychotherapy, our studies at Vassar have shown a statistical trend for college students to become more independent in their judgment between freshman and senior years. Many factors within the college contribute to this outcome, but I believe that one necessary condition is a meaningful relationship with at least one member of the faculty, for only an admired adult can stand against the values of the student's peers and those of his parents.

14

Uses of the Senior Year

Some time ago, I was invited to talk to the "sponsors" at Stanford. They are seniors who have agreed to help indoctrinate freshmen in the local mythology and lore and whatever else freshmen need to be indoctrinated into. The sponsors function during orientation week, meeting the freshmen and then taking the role of big brother or big sister throughout their first year of college. It seemed appropriate, therefore, to say something about freshmen as I have understood them. So I spoke of the freshman's instability with respect to self-esteem, of his susceptibility to authoritarian attitudes and to influence by the friendship groups to which he belonged early in his college career. I asserted that, as a rule, the freshman is bound to his peer group not so much by ties of friendship as by fear of how he would be regarded should he leave it, that, indeed, membership in the peer group is commonly constricting and that, in order for a student to develop as an individual, he often must free himself from his group membership.

At the conclusion of the talk, the chairman invited questions. We didn't get any. I was a little hurt because I thought my material should have been of interest to the students.

At last, there was a question, a common one: "Don't you think too much introspection might not be a good thing for students?" This, of course, presented an opportunity to tell about the Vassar girls who had taken part in our research and who had introspected like crazy for four years and who seemed to flourish under that program. There were no more questions, and the meeting broke up.

Feeling some need to bolster my ego, I recalled the sober attentiveness of the audience and told myself that the trouble was probably that the things I was saying were a little too close to home, that the students didn't want to ask questions because they were afraid they might reveal themselves more than seemed appropriate. Happily, I was able to confirm this hypothesis a couple of weeks later, when I had another meeting with some of the sponsors in an informal situation. Now there were many questions, but they were mainly about the situation of the senior rather than about that of the freshman. I now believe that on the occasion of the talk, when I tried to say how life really is on the campus, the seniors were not thinking about freshmen; they were thinking about themselves as individuals who were still quite possibly in need of further development; and they were thinking back to some of their own experiences in college and wondering whether it might not still be possible to make more of their remaining opportunities.

This experience with the student sponsors led me to the suggestions that I want to make later on. Suffice it to say now that when we plan the total educational environment, we should do so with attention to the special opportunities of senior year.

Planning an educational environment must be guided by some theory of personality as well as by social theory. In order to connect observations of behavior in residences and observations of behavior in the classroom, we need a theory of the whole person. It is through observing behavior in a diversity of situations that we may infer central trends in the personality, and it is on the basis of these trends that we can make hypotheses concerning the effectiveness of institutional arrangements for inducing the kinds of behavior we are interested in. We need a theory that will tell us which parts or aspects of the person are determinative with respect to other parts, and that will give us some notion as to which parts of the personality are open to influence by forces arising outside. We also need social theory from which we can derive hypotheses about how to arrange the social environment in ways that permit stimuli to reach those parts of the personality which determine change in the whole. And because students, like all people, change over time, we must take into account the developmental status of those for whom we arrange a college environment.

All education can utilize knowledge about how people develop, but personality theory has a special relevance to general education. At this time of wanton specialization, general education hardly needs to be defended, but there may be differences in how the term is understood. For me, general education means more than the philosophy that students should know something about this, that, and the other, or should have some familiarity with certain characteristic phenomena of our culture; it means the kind of education that develops the individual.

It has been said that general education is concerned with what remains when the content of courses is forgotten. The reference here must be to certain qualities of the person, certain general skills, certain kinds of powers, perhaps certain intellectual tools that exist independently of particular kinds of subject matter. It is general and durable qualities of this kind that will serve the individual best in the diversity of situations in which he will find himself as he goes through life, that will make him able to deal with the changes that are bound to occur within any specialty that he might enter.

Examples of purely intellectual powers would be those of analysis, synthesis, and generalization. But if we think of the demands upon the individual in the world of today and of what it takes to meet them, we are easily led to consider even more general qualities. For example, because we cannot any longer think of educating people for particular social or vocational roles, knowing (as we do) that they are going to be called upon to take a great many *different* roles, we must think in terms of developing the kind of flexibility that will permit individuals to move easily from one role to another and to perform well in each of them.

This flexibility is more than a mere behavioral trait,

like friendliness, or a special skill that may simply be added to a person. It is an abstracted feature of the whole personality. Qualities such as flexibility, independence of thinking, or mature social responsibility do not exist at birth, nor do they exist as a rule in the college freshman. They have to be developed; and they do develop under conditions that we can learn to understand and, within limits, to control. These qualities develop together: so closely are they interrelated that a change in one will bring change in others. On this basis, one can say that a central purpose of higher education is the fullest possible development of the whole personality, a purpose that ought to be served by every aspect of the college environment. The curriculum, methods of teaching, the organization of teacher-student relationships, living arrangements, extracurricular activities, activities of the president and his assistants—all should be studied anew, with attention to how they may contribute to individual development.

I am aware that this accent on the theory of personality can easily lead to some misunderstanding, such as the common if misleading distinction between "personality" and "intellect." One reason for such a distinction seems to be our practice of referring to personality *traits;* hence, personality comes to be thought of as an aggregate of observable components. For example, it is likely that some of us conceive of *authoritarianism* as a trait of personality, as a characteristic we might ascribe to a person after observing a particular pattern of social behavior, just as we speak of a student's skepticism on the basis of familiarity with his intellectual performances. This is a misleading view of the matter. All traits, intellectual or other, are traits of personality, but authoritarianism is not a trait. It is a hypothetical construct standing for a complex of forces deep within the personality, not a kind of behavior that can be observed directly. Authoritarianism is, to be sure, expressed in behavior, but its manifestations are often so subtle, indirect, and diversified that its measurement requires special instruments and observation by highly trained psychologists.

Authoritarianism is but one of many conceptions that go to make up the technical baggage of the personality theorists. This technical baggage should not be a source of pride. If we knew enough, we would probably be able to have our say simply and in plain language. But given the task of explaining consistent behavior, of finding connections among apparently unrelated surface events, we must use hypothetical constructs, invent terms, and do a certain amount of talking to ourselves. But in speaking of the everyday behavior of students, particularly of those kinds of behavior that must be evaluated, we can just as well use ordinary words. For example, my favorite terms from the Vassar work—"authoritarianism," "impulse expression," "developmental status," and the like—could be translated into terms of ability. In addition to familiar intellectual and artistic abilities, we could speak of the ability to achieve accurate social perceptions, the ability to see oneself as others do, the ability to control one's emotional impulses, and so on.

I want now to consider briefly a case that may illustrate something of what I mean. I am thinking of a young woman whom I knew well as she went through college and who changed radically over the four-year period. As a freshman, she was a perfect example of what we used to call the peer-group-oriented girl. She arrived at college in the company of friends whom she had known at school, and had arranged to room with some of these girls, on a corridor with other girls like them. She and some of her friends spent the first evening at college playing bridge in comfort and relaxation, feeling that they had already mastered this new situation and probably could master others, without being changed by them. They exhibited what might be called the "private-school girl's complex," a personality configuration marked by a sense of superiority to most other people, a readiness to abide by the strict discipline of the school when external control is needed but to ignore it in favor of their own group norms when it seems safe to do so, and an inclination to look at college-going as an expression of status rather than as a means for personal development. In their relations with adults these girls are polite, poised, well-behaved; they do exactly what is expected but no more, and they thus keep the faculty at a distance and ensure that they will not really be touched by the educational offerings of the college.

Knowing many such girls, I expected little of our subject. It turned out, however, that by senior year she had changed radically according to our test scores. From being relatively high on authoritarianism as a freshman, she had moved to a position in the lowest quarter of her class; and from being low on the expression of impulses in behavior or in conscious fantasy, she had moved from the lowest quarter of her class to the highest. She was very much aware of changes in herself and could describe them convincingly. A girl who appeared in the beginning to be rather unpromising as a scholar, she had now taken hold in a social science discipline and been offered a most attractive fellowship for graduate study.

Asked what had caused the change, she said, "Well, it was all due to Mr. A.," a teacher who was able to relate his material to matters that were of genuine interest and concern to the girls, to hitch his world onto theirs in a way that made both come alive. Our subject often felt that he was really talking to her and about things that were close to the center of her major preoccupations. He was undoubtedly an attractive chap, less in physical appearance than in his enthusiasm and magnetism and in his willingness to reveal himself as a person. He was often seen about the campus at the center of a group of girls, one of whom was usually our subject.

The time came when the students discovered that this teacher's contract was not going to be renewed. Our subject was one of a group of girls who now worked for his retention, circulating a petition and interviewing numerous faculty members and administrators. She had found a hero and a cause. It was a dramatic and thorough involvement and became the basis for change in this girl's relationships with her peers. She was able to break away from the rather constricting peer culture in which she had been submerged for two and a half years. Because of her attachment to an adult whose authority could be set in opposition to what her fellow students stood for, it was now possible for her to support a break from them on the basis of her own intelligence and knowledge. With these processes at work in our subject, she could look elsewhere for friends and relationships. She made an entirely new set of friends, who supported the new value system that she acquired through her relationship with Mr. A. And because her relationship with this one teacher opened the way to all teachers, she was able to have essentially equalitarian relationships with a number of them.

It is important to note that, in our subject's psychological household, her peer group had essentially the same role that her parents once had. The peer group provided the emotional support for values and beliefs that had been acquired automatically in childhood and sustained by family and the local community. It is because the peer group represents the traditional value system that its influence can be countered only by adults—singly or in community—and by the developing self-awareness and critical power of the student himself. It should be noted, too, that this was a drama of the intellect and of the spirit. There was never any reference to the physical attractiveness of Mr. A., although our subject made it clear that she liked both him and his wife. Everything was played out in the realms of intellectual interest and controversy; and one might say that this made the whole affair all the more passionate.

The moral of my story is that a student's behavior in respect to his social group and to student culture, his relationships with his teachers, his behavior in the classroom, and his reactions to the content of courses are all closely related; they are related in the sense that they all express, and are in part determined by, the same organization of underlying processes in the personality. To further the understanding of these processes and their manifestations in behavior is the function of personality theory.

Let us take another example. At a southern college some of the faculty and I were talking about authoritarianism and how it might be reduced by educational means. As one technique, I suggested teaching people to think in quantitative terms, in terms of variability, probability, and the like, thus making it possible for them to avoid hackneyed verbal categories. This led one of the teachers to say to me later that she had now a fresh appreciation of the possibilities in lecturing. She explained that she taught psychological statistics and had felt that many of the students were not getting it and that most of the others could take it or leave it alone. But one day, after a class in which she had been lecturing on probability, she encountered one of her students in a corner, crying. This young woman was willing to talk to a sympathetic listener, and it turned out that she was crying because, as she said, she didn't know what to think any longer. She felt that her whole belief system was crumbling. She may have come to realize that if she went along with this teacher and thought about quantitative distinctions among things, or about human variability, or in terms of what was probably true and probably untrue, she would have to give up those rigid categories which up until now she had used in facing the world.

This is saying, I think, that an intellectual change can ramify throughout the whole personality and initiate changes in fundamental structures. If it is really true that a person with an authoritarian personality structure has difficulty in learning certain aspects of mathematics and science, it is also true that if one succeeds in teaching some mathematics and science to some students, one can thereby modify an authoritarian structure in the personality.

I want to come now to some consideration of the senior. In planning a senior center or other programs for seniors, we should take fully into account what the senior is like. Obviously, his responses to our plans and undertakings will depend in considerable part upon what is going on within him.

In the first place, it is well to remember that the senior is in many important ways like all other people. He certainly develops in accordance with principles that hold generally. He, like everyone else, is open to further development, and whether or not he *does* develop will depend upon the conditions that are brought to bear. Again, in seniors as in other people, development is progressive. There is an order of events according to which certain things have to happen before other things become possible. For a developmental change to occur, there must be a certain readiness, but the change requires not only the existence of that readiness by itself but also some kind of intervention from outside.

On the basis of research at Vassar, we reported that seniors as compared with lower classmen are more sophisticated, more flexible in thinking, more tolerant, freer in the use of imagination—to mention only a few differentiating characteristics. For our present purposes, the important thing to note is that curves representing developmental change in college tend to level off after the beginning of the junior year, suggesting that most of what happens developmentally in college happens during the first two years, and that a little more happens in the third year than in the fourth. This seems to mean that students become adapted to the college. They have learned the ropes; and after a couple of years they get to a place where challenges are not sufficient to induce developmental changes. The phenomenon is most pronounced in seniors, who, as far as development is concerned, appear to be resting on their laurels.

There is also evidence, mainly from studies of young women, that the leveling off that begins in the junior year tends to persist during the first four or five years after graduation from college. This suggests the possibility that once a person has entered the world of affairs and accepted the responsibilities of a job and a family, it is difficult to develop further because social roles require a conformity increasingly hard to challenge. If this is so, senior year is a sort of last chance now being widely lost.

This opportunity could be turned to advantage, however, by a wide variety of programs. Seniors who are relatively free of authoritarianism might be appropriately challenged by helping to orient and counsel freshmen. I have several things in mind. If seniors became expert in the sociology and social psychology of their own colleges, they could pass this knowledge along to entering freshmen. They, of course, offer this kind of instruction anyway, though usually interlarded with their own cynicism. I am suggesting not that seniors should simply adopt our values and dogmas and pass these along to freshmen, but that they should take part in an intellectual analysis of what goes on at the college, and in the communication of this knowledge to freshmen.

Working with faculty and others, seniors should become familiar with the new literature on college peer groups, student culture, student-faculty relations, what the administration is up against or up to, how the curriculum is made. Let them be wise men in the eyes of the freshmen, but let their reputations be based on knowledge derived from systematic study of the college community and from efforts to understand the processes of their own education. If we move far enough in this direction, everything about the college can become the object of intellectual analysis; and we can reduce the usual barriers between the academic, which is sometimes called intellectual, and the other activities of the college. In thinking of how to link the seniors and freshmen on the same campus, I am proposing a kind of campus Peace Corps, in which some members of a community take it upon themselves to help other members. Seniors may tutor freshmen or participate in seminars or discussions, showing freshmen how educated men conduct themselves in these settings. I am not thinking here primarily of helping freshmen or of helping faculty with their enormous teaching burden; I am thinking rather of helping seniors. The example offered in the beginning of this chapter was intended to suggest that if we invite seniors to worry about freshmen, they gain a new awareness of themselves. Like the mother who relives her adolescence through that of her daughter, the senior who works closely with freshmen will recall his own freshman self; he will see it in a new light and incorporate this new conception into his personality.

Meanwhile, his relationships with faculty members would probably deepen. It has often been said that students never understand their teachers until they become teachers themselves. We can speed the process of understanding by giving seniors a taste of colleagueship, a sense of what it means to participate as equals in the work of the faculty.

If we arrange things so that the intellectual activities of students really contribute something to the community in which they live—rather than stand as the means by which they advance themselves at the expense of their friends—we would at once promote the intellectual life and the values of decency and social responsibility. The intellectual in our society is much too alienated from his community and much too defensive in consequence. Feeling that he is not understood or appreciated, he mutters contemptuously about "togetherness" and sinks more deeply into isolation and meanness. I think this is most likely to happen to a person who has never had an experience in which his best intellectual endeavor became a part of a group enterprise, where its social meaning and relevance could become apparent to him. I would like to see us, therefore, create situations in which the more able and advanced students can be helpful to some of their fellows. Perhaps we may thus reduce somewhat the purely competitive and self-seeking aspects of our educational system. And perhaps we may thus develop in students the sense of social responsibility on which, in turn, the community depends.

James Coleman (1959) has noted our difficulty in contriving arrangements in which intellectual endeavors are carried out by teams or accompanied by a group spirit. Research work does, of course, often have this aspect, but it is rare that undergraduates are able to take part in it. Perhaps those who work on the school paper learn something of intellectual cooperation, but by and large, in hard academic work it is every man for himself. Probably our accent on free enterprise serves our need to evaluate and allocate students better than it serves our purpose of educating them.

This leads me to wonder why fraternities are so persistent, why they don't just give up in the face of all the opposition and criticism they encounter. Do they serve needs other than those for status and exclusiveness? For many students, surely, the need to have close associates who can be trusted, and for whom sacrifices can be made, is very strong.

I was reminded of this on a visit to the South, where I became very much aware once again of the clash of cultures in this country. In the South, the human community is still very much alive and enormously important. People are accepted and valued unconditionally; the black sheep or underachiever is not rejected; family solidarity, friendship, fraternity still matter a great deal, often more than success or status. There is still a sharp contrast with Yankee mercantilism—the hard-headed, hard-bargaining, puritanical, competitive system in which people as well as things are evaluated in terms of what they can be exchanged for. Nowhere is the old Yankee spirit more persistent than in northern colleges and universities, the last of the nineteenth-century "enterprises," where, as Howard Becker has pointed out, grades have for students the functions of money in the larger society and where the marketable professor is the one who publishes. What the Southern states are to the whole body politic, the fraternities are to the colleges and universities. Probably the Civil War is not really going to be won; but we may hope for a synthesis that embodies the best elements of the two cultures.

One way to deal with the fraternities is to make them the scenes of our strongest efforts to create intellectual communities, of experiments in the integration of living and learning. I would just as soon start with the fraternity as with any other group, winning the cooperation of its leadership, inviting them to help educate the younger members and thus to build a community of teacher-learners.

15

The Neglected Art of College Teaching

One way to understand the importance of college teaching is to ask some recent graduates, "What was the most significant thing that happened to you in college?" The chances are good that in one way or another their key experience involved a teacher.

When I put this question recently to a young alumna of one of our women's colleges, she recalled two experiences that were very important to her. The first was a freshman seminar in which the teacher made her feel that what she had to say was being listened to and was a worthwhile contribution to the group. It was here that she first learned to value the use of the mind; she developed a commitment to her education and became an *A* student. The second experience occurred in her senior year. A professor had assigned a difficult paper, which she completed and turned in, fully expecting her usual *A*. But the paper was returned with a grade of *D*. When she inquired the reason, the professor spent a long time pointing out the weaknesses of the work —"about an hour on the first page, another on the second, and so on." By page three this young woman had learned a great deal about humility, about what it takes to do good work, and about what a teacher can do for a student.

Effective teaching is an art, one of the highest and most important arts we have. Consider, for example, what a large range of things the teacher needs to know. First, he must know about students—the differences among them and among their needs at different times. At one time, a little encouragement from someone may determine whether a young person becomes a scholar, or even whether he stays in college. At another time, he may need to have his deficiencies revealed, to be brought up short and told how to do better.

A good teacher must also know when to keep quiet and how to create an atmosphere in which students feel like talking because they know they will neither be laughed at nor punished for what they say. He must also know how to evaluate work, which means he must be a master of his own discipline. He must know how to offer criticism in a way that students can accept. Perhaps most of all, he must be a person who is respected and admired by students; who has convinced them that what he does is not just for his own personal satisfaction, but for them.

A truly liberal education, as we define it here, seeks to develop certain qualities within the person: an ability to think well and independently, a disposition to inquire into matters and to know how the inquiry can most effectively be carried out, an awareness and understanding of self, a capacity to respond to the manifold aspects of our culture, a sense of responsibility for the well-being of society.

The development of these qualities depends less upon the quantity of facts acquired than upon the purposes and style of teachers. When they fail as catalysts of change, the student might as well be learning his facts from teaching machines or independently from books. What he needs, however, is a challenge not only to his reading speed and memory but also to the values that he learned at Mother's knee and later in his peer group. Some of these values will be shaken by the challenge and others strengthened by having gone through it.

In examining what is worth doing and having, the

student needs from his teachers the support for free inquiry which is so often lacking from his family and home community. The best support is an example to follow, a model of inquiry to emulate. In order to make the student dissatisfied with the unexamined notions he typically brings to college, the teacher must reveal himself, instead of hiding behind lecture notes. He must feel free to expose his ignorance as well as his erudition, to show his feelings and to invite discussion on topics about which everyone feels strongly. How else can he show students how to differ with people in a civilized way, with intellect as well as passion? If the teacher exposes his own humanity, he will begin to see his students as human beings, too; as people who need to be drawn out, heard, and encouraged.

In recent years we have been hearing sad stories about the decline in the art of teaching and the consequent deterioration in student-faculty relations. In the large universities particularly, students and faculty know less and less of each other. Students have come to expect this and often do not even take advantage of the office hours that are offered; they feel that the professor probably will not be interested anyway. Frequently the relationship is so remote that students cannot even describe their teachers as people. In a questionnaire for freshmen at Stanford we asked students to describe some of their teachers. The boys simply could not do it: they made a few remarks about the teacher as a teacher, but they had no conception of him as a person. The girls did only slightly better. To these students, a professor appears to be little more than a lecturer who comes and talks for 50 minutes and then disappears. As they saw it, their sole task was to get information down on paper. Faculty members, in turn, often think that students are mainly seeking entertainment and a way to "beat the system." If they come up to talk after class, teachers suspect it is only to be noticed and to get a better grade. As the faculty seek to minimize student disruption of their intricate professional schedules, and as students come to worry mainly about admission to graduate school, each side confirms the other's expectations.

This decline in teaching is commonly explained in terms of "explosions" in number of students, in amount of knowledge, and in the potential for war. To a degree these explanations are valid.

In order to cope with the great influx of students into our institutions of higher learning in the last decade, we have organized colleges like factories run by bureaucracies. Meanwhile, as research has become organized in a similar way, faculties are overwhelmed by the accumulation of papers and books which they feel must somehow be covered. As a result, many courses are taught not because they are a part of a well thought-out curriculum but because some individual teacher thinks that the subject is important, and was assured on recruitment that he could teach a course in it.

The Cold War, too, has affected higher education. The announcement of the first Russian Sputnik marked the beginning of the current emphasis on vocational training and on preparation for specialized careers, to the detriment of the aims of liberal education. More and more, colleges have come to resemble graduate schools. As a research specialist, the college teacher has the same interests as his colleagues in graduate school and naturally seeks to make his students resemble graduate students as early as possible, to the neglect of their general development.

In this situation, teaching becomes a lost art, which professors have no motive to learn and students therefore lack a model of. Parents, and no doubt others, think of education primarily as a matter of taking courses, learning content, taking examinations, and getting grades. Who perpetuates this view? I am afraid that the faculties and administrations of colleges have themselves done much to spread it. Perhaps psychologists have contributed as well by treating learning as the simple accretion of more and more bits of information. Most of the psychology of learning deals only with how content is registered and remembered, failing to recognize that education really has more to do with unlearning, with motivation, and with relationships with teachers than with recall of facts. One of the most important functions of education is to erase wrong attitudes acquired in earlier periods, something that cannot be done simply by superimposing more knowledge on the wrong foundations that happen already to have been set up. Similarly, most teacher training in schools of education has proceeded on the assumption that teachers are mainly transmitters of information. They are accordingly taught the skills needed to pass content from books or personal experience into the minds of students. But they learn little that will equip them with the sensitivity shown by the teacher of our young alumna's freshman seminar or the professor who criticized her senior paper.

Of course, the schools of education produce chiefly elementary and secondary teachers. The average college teacher is even more poorly prepared. Graduate schools, from which college teachers come, pay almost no attention to teaching; they fill the student's time with specialized courses and assume that if he can earn his Ph.D., he can teach, or else that he will not have to teach. And it is next to impossible to persuade a graduate student in history or sociology or psychology to take a course in the school of education. Stipends are available for graduate students who are willing to learn something about teaching while working toward their Ph.D.s, but these stipends are not being picked up with enthusiasm. Students seem afraid that education courses might corrupt them or lower their status. Consequently, the various seminars in higher education—which would seem to have significance for any graduate student who expects to teach in college—are usually attended only by students from the school of education.

If we hope to improve things, we must consider teaching as the art that it is. It is surprising to find that, in spite of the deteriorating situation, members of college faculties seldom talk about teaching—about what it is like to be in a classroom, what one is there to do, or how one deals with this or that situation. They seldom mention the times when they wonder why they are there at all—and perhaps wish that they were not.

We may wonder what will happen when parents, who foot the bill for education, find out what is really happening in the classrooms. Many of their young people already know, and we can hear them say at the end of the quarter, "Another $450 down the drain." These students have some conception of what they should be getting out of college, and they suspect that they are not getting it in their four lecture courses, taught by four impersonal professors, who hand out information in a routine way.

Certainly as students and parents learn more about education, the demands on teachers are bound to increase. And there are some other hopeful signs that teaching may eventually be restored to its rightful place: teaching machines may show that information can be handed out by means other than the live lecture, and educational television may bring the best lectures to more students and thus force other teachers to become good discussion leaders, and good tutors, rather than lecturers.

Some efforts are already being made to improve teaching. The whole design for the Santa Cruz Campus of the University of California is an attempt to create a climate in which teachers will become interested in students and will have an opportunity really to teach them. Berkeley has at last been able to launch an experimental program (see Chapter 4). In this program five teachers are responsible for the first two years' education of 150 self-selected students, which is the same student-teacher ratio as in the undergraduate division as a whole. Directed by Professor Joseph Tussman of the philosophy department, this is a program without courses. The entire curriculum consists of the study of a series of crises in civilization, from the Greeks through seventeenth-century England to the United States of the present, with provision for one course to be taken outside. Most of the teaching is in seminars and in conferences with individual students, with weekly meetings of the whole "college" for lectures or discussions. Once the idea of the course had been abandoned, it became possible to experiment with various methods of teaching. It was quite an achievement for Professor Tussman to convince the faculty at Berkeley that students in this experimental program would probably be able to compete in upper-division courses with those who had been exposed to elementary courses in a variety of disciplines.

Other, less dramatic arrangements are being made elsewhere to provide more communication between students and teachers. At Stanford, for instance, there is increasing pressure on teachers to have more lunches in the residence halls and more evening discussions with students in the lounges. It has been proposed that we offer courses in the residence halls, so that living and learning can be brought more closely together. Arrangements of this kind are based on the assumption that the student will get as much from what the teacher *is* as from what he presents in content.

If we accept this position (and many Americans do not), we have no choice but to make arrangements for students to know teachers and teachers to know students. This is one of the benefits of a smaller college or a specialized educational setting. Students returning from the foreign campuses of Stanford, for example, bring with them a great nostalgia for the happy days they spent there. In those relatively small communities abroad, many learned for the first time what intellectual fellowship is and how rewarding a teacher can be when he is encouraged to reveal himself as a person. Students have an opportunity to see him in a variety of roles—as husband, father, traveling companion, gourmet, connoisseur of the arts, and member of a complex human community. The teacher who manages to pass these tests as a person has students who learn from him in the classroom. Small wonder that students returning from Stanford-in-France ask, "Why can't we have a Stanford-in-Palo Alto?"

This kind of personal relationship is not so easy to achieve on American campuses under pressure of limited time and of an apparently unlimited number of students wanting to be educated. But it may yet be possible if we are willing to deemphasize content and agree that we need not try to "cover" so much, provided we teach well. What matters is what happens in the student's mind. With this approach, we may find the courage to experiment radically with how to use the time we spend with students. It is, after all, not the amount of time we spend with students that is crucial, but the conditions under which we spend it. With a little imagination, I am sure we can devise situations in which they will be more receptive than in the usual rut of day-in-day-out class attendance. We might, for example, bring groups of students who do not know one another together for weekend seminars. The change in the situation would force them to change their ways of adapting to one another, thus opening them to experience. They might learn as much in one weekend as in an entire semester of conventional class lectures.

The mere fact that a teacher is interested in teaching, and is willing to try new methods, has a good effect on students today. At one time I was asked to consult with members of a university department who were preparing to compare the gains from different methods of teaching—the lecture, discusssion, and simulated decision making (a procedure according to which a class might, for example, put themselves in the place of a committee of the U. S. Senate). Since similar studies have for years been producing widely varying results, I was not too excited about the research itself; but I was interested in the effect that talk about doing an experiment was having on the students involved. I was told that in the year since the planning of the study had begun, enrollment in the department had doubled—making this department the second largest in the university. Students had evidently found that these particular teachers were interested in teaching, and accordingly they flocked to the classes. We might say that this educational experiment was already a success before the grant proposal was ever submitted. The benefits of research flow from two sources—from the knowledge that is ultimately gained and from the excitement generated by the doing of the research. Katz and Korn (1966) have produced evidence to suggest that there may be no better way to interest teachers in students than to involve them in a research project to study student reaction to their classes.

Another good device for interesting teachers in students is to have them attempt some counseling. Perhaps a teacher should continue to counsel the same students over their four years in college, so that he can get to know some of them as individuals. If he gets to know even a few of them well, his attitude toward students in general will change. When he faces a class, he will see it as a group of individuals—not just a mass indistinguishable from last year's.

Much as they deserve our applause, all these measures are still regarded as luxuries to be paid for with "outside" money. The new look which they imply has not really penetrated the core of the educational enterprise, but when it does—and I am hopeful that it will soon—we will look upon the teacher in a very different way: not just as a skilled professional but as a leader of society. For the person who has the responsibility for bringing up youth must be more than a technician or a genteel servant or a bureaucrat. He must know a lot about youth, through studying them intensively, in school and out, and about the aims of our society in accordance with which youth are currently brought up. From his own education he must be a person who knows how to make value judgments, who knows the important issues and is not afraid to discuss them with students, or to take positions on national problems, on taste, and on morals in the various areas of our lives.

16

The Size
and Coherence
of the University

When someone mentions the problem of size in a college, we are likely to think immediately of such giant universities as Berkeley or Ohio State. What troubles us, however, is not size as such, but lack of coherence. In a liberal-arts college where everyone is at least acquainted with nearly everyone else, an expansion to a total of 600 students might threaten the community's coherence; but in certain major universities, that entire number could be added to the enrollment with few harmful effects. The point is that coherence depends not on size alone, but on leadership, internal structure, and the educational style of the college. The University of Minnesota, for instance, has a very large enrollment, but a visitor can sense that its elements somehow pull together. In the same way, Berkeley in 1940 had 20,000 students, or nearly as many as today, but to those of us who taught there, it did not seem too large: we felt that the university was still of one piece, that its leaders spoke for it as a whole, and that everybody was somehow identified with the total enterprise.

In evaluating a college or university, we should thus avoid confusing size and coherence. Each size has its own virtues. Certain styles of development require the community of a small school; others thrive more readily in the rich and diverse environment provided by a major university.

As an organism or social system grows larger, its survival requires a differentiation of functions; and as the complexity increases, its coherence depends upon the integration of its new variety of functions. In higher education as elsewhere, the problem is to hold together while keeping up. Although a few universities are resisting the pressure for larger enrollments, the question for most is not *whether* to grow but *how*—according to what pattern. Assuming, for example, that Stanford will grow, should it become like Berkeley or like Princeton? Should it emphasize graduate education and research or try also to retain the traditional values of the liberal university, with at least as much accent on undergraduate as on graduate education? These questions are complicated by pressures other than enrollment—such pressures as the growth of detailed knowledge, the resulting proliferation of courses, the increasing specialization and isolation of departments, and the division of effort between teaching and research.

The practical results of increasing complexity are familiar on our campuses. The more students there are, the more disconnected they tend to be from each other, from the faculty, and from the administration. Attending larger classes, a student has less opportunity to know his teachers; and dealing with a largely impersonal bureaucracy, he is taught to regard himself less as a person than as a set of responses to institutional requirements. Instead of getting to know an admired adult, he is dealt with by offices in charge of such functions as registration, counseling, teaching, and discipline—all according to a model adapted from business and the military. To the people who perform these functions, students appear less as individuals than as "problems" in the areas handled by each office. Conversely, the student is rarely able to deal with adults as individuals. Observing his busy professors in a variety of roles—as lecturers, as committee members, and so forth—the student is impressed by their inconsistency.

Still another complicating factor in a large university is the enormous diversity of needs and interests that exists among the people within it and among those outside who expect something from it. The government is providing an increasingly large fraction of the university budget, for the support of research and of specialized training which it considers important. Inside the universities, life often appears to be every man for himself, with each department, institute, center, or agency focused on its own special interests. One is forced to ask whether there are any general purposes of the whole institution and, if so, who is looking after them.

Among the most promising sources of educational purpose are the better of our small liberal-arts colleges. With the freedom to experiment, they can deliberately choose to prove the virtues of community rather than merely to ape the glamour-seeking of their larger brothers. In this way, as in others, a private college could serve as a model that even public institutions may in time want to follow. One model badly in need of representation is that of education for the development of the whole person, not just of those peculiar skills which assure his admission to graduate school. For our own sons and daughters, we want a college that will help them become persons of character as well as of intellect; and when we apply this ideal to other people's children as well, we are moving toward the conception of an aristocratic education for everybody.

Another way of putting the case for general education of the individual is to ask what is required for citizenship in the country and in the entire world today. Students must learn not only what minimal duty they owe to society, as in the usual civics class, but also how to resist pressures to conform and how to think independently. A small liberal-arts college can teach independence by its own example, by its freedom from state control, its ability to foster minority ideas and to criticize the prevailing wisdom. Even though graduates of such colleges are relatively few, they act as social leaven, supporting with their character, as foundations do with money, a variety of new and hopeful social patterns.

Largeness and complexity, however, are very much with us. Neither is an evil in itself. The problem is that as colleges and universities have grown, complexity has begun to outrun integration. Meanwhile, traditional means of holding the university together are breaking down: as higher education becomes financially available to a wider socioeconomic range, the student body becomes less homogeneous; and as dormitory capacity is exceeded, a declining proportion of college students are living on campus. Teacher-student contacts are diminishing—partly as a result of the very differentiating forces which, ironically, we would hope such contacts could mitigate. Leisure has all but vanished under the pressure of demands for excellence, even though free time is essential for making friends and for sorting through the confusing diversity of college life. In the midst of such academic incoherence, we need to strengthen the forces of integration.

The Recovery of Purpose.   Instead of keeping a clear idea of what they exist to do, universities have sometimes acted as if their main purpose were to survive, and as if the key to survival were frenetic attendance to the interests of as many different groups as possible. In doing so, they have forgotten that the parts of a college, as of a university, have little in common except the undergraduates —students so unsophisticated as to presume upon more than a single department. Faced with this legion of polymorphs, the various departments and offices assemble only to set rules, to revise the curriculum, and to discuss what can possibly be done about discipline. In the absence of undergraduates, what would bring the departments together? Today's scholars and their graduate students are seldom so frivolous as to wander beyond the precinct of their own chosen discipline. In view of this regard for the law of trespass, departments are forced to stay near one another not, as some would say, by a common need for the computation center (which dataphones can now reach from afar), but primarily by the demands of undergraduate education. The degree to which these demands are met is reflected in studies we have conducted at Vassar and, more recently, at Berkeley and Stanford. By interviewing a large sample of students several times each year during their college careers, we learned that institutional coherence and the strength of peer culture vary inversely. When faced with fragmentation among the adults, students turn more exclusively to each other; but when shown a larger purpose, they know how to respond.

Generalism.   Many of the disintegrating forces at work

in universities can be traced to the way in which the search for knowledge is currently organized. As the departments become more highly specialized, the typical faculty member is increasingly absorbed in research problems difficult to connect with his teaching. If you want to embarrass a young scholar, ask him the subject of his Ph.D. dissertation: he is probably unable to tell a layman in plain language what it was about, and he suspects that, even if he could, the layman would regard the subject as trivial—a thought probably entertained by the scholar as well. To advance in his discipline, however, the young professor is forced to specialize, leaving most of the larger questions to old men and undergraduates. To provide for the latter group, the college may try to cajole its specialists away from their furrows and back, for at least a few hours each week, to the field of general education courses. More to the point, colleges could begin to reward not only the usual reports of "original research" but also the publication of essays significant to undergraduates and even possibly to scholars across the disciplinary fence.

One approach to generalizing inquiry, at least in the social sciences, is through multidisciplinary research institutes, where problems are defined according to their human significance. Problems such as human destructiveness, alcoholism, and the general disaffection of youth appear in different forms from time to time, and must be met on their own terms, not as partial illustrations of pre-existing disciplines. These are problems that everybody can worry about and, up to a point, understand; and staff members of our Institute for the Study of Human Problems at Stanford have found that even freshmen are interested and able to take part in the research or field work.

Subdivision. Students need coherence within the college society as well as within the intellectual issues they deal with. For a number of years I have been advocating the division of universities into smaller colleges such as those now being built at the new campus of the University of California at Santa Cruz. Its plan calls for a set of colleges of no more than about 700 students each, within a total university that will also include some graduate divisions. All the colleges will share the library facilities and some of the science laboratories. It is hoped that having smaller colleges will make it possible once again for professors and students to know each other, and for the students to become better acquainted.

It is true that the Santa Cruz project has the advantage of being newly begun, but why cannot we do something of this kind in existing institutions? If education is to have the developmental influence that we hope for, it should be carried out in a community: a student must feel he knows of or *could* know nearly everyone else. For this purpose, an enrollment of 600 may represent the upper limit, even though each class would thus have only 150. As Newcomb (1962) has shown, mutual familiarity is also necessary for the transfer of faculty values to student culture.

Until a few years ago a well-known college enrolled only about 200 students and contained a single student-faculty culture. Entering freshmen would soon discover they had no alternative to joining it. Then somebody donated enough money to build a new dormitory, and subsequently 100 freshmen were admitted, all at once. Since the faculty and students who were already there could not get to know them fast enough, these freshmen proceeded to generate a subculture of their own, rather different from what the authorities would have preferred.

In general, a college should be neither too large for security nor too small for diversity. The actual size depends on such factors as location and social style. Riesman and Jencks (1962) suggest that alone in the countryside a college of 700 might lack sufficient diversity, but that within a university or an exciting city, a college of 300 or 400 would be ideal. Amusingly, they suggest that 450 is too big for a "house" at Harvard, where students tend to withdraw into their shells, but not for a college in the more sociable atmosphere of Yale.

The ideal size also varies inversely with the variety of the students admitted. If the group is heterogeneous, a smaller number would allow people to get to know one another more easily; but if it is less various, a larger number would help to increase the diversity. Similarly, if all students share a single curriculum, the institution can safely be larger than if they do not, for a core of common learning tends to pull them together. What the student needs is the social support of a group that is sharing his attempt to re-examine values and to entertain ideas seldom thought about—or even opposed— back home.

Community. The counseling system suggests one means of integration less drastic than subdividing the university. Once at Berkeley we had a policy that each faculty member would counsel 25 freshmen. In my own experience under this system, I was struck by how easy it was to avoid establishing any relationship with a student: if I stuck strictly to the business of signing the study list and suggesting that he read the catalogue, I could be rid of him in five minutes. The whole situation would change, however, when I asked him a question about himself, about how he had spent the summer or what he really wanted to do with himself. I had the sad experience of hearing a young man recall years later that only during his freshman interview did he ever find a professor who was interested in him. If a relationship of that quality could be maintained during four years, it could promote student development by increasing the continuity of college experience.

In the course of our research on undergraduates, we have discovered that if you interview a student each year, asking personal questions about what he is doing, what he is interested in, and the like, you will find that he feels some obligation to make what he says one year consistent with what he said the year before. And by the time these students get to be seniors, they regard being research subjects as the most important thing that has happened to them in college. At Stanford, where we have just finished such a program with 100 students, we found that saying good-bye before graduation in June was a moving experience for both the students and the research staff. Students had gradually formed attachments to their interviewers and to their place within the research program, and the interviewers had, in turn, formed attachments to the students. In view of the benefits which this program yielded to everyone concerned, colleges might seriously consider conducting interviews of this kind regularly with all students.

Another result of such programs is a demonstration to the faculty that relationships with students are not necessarily too costly in time and emotion. Like physicians, most teachers assume that if they interest themselves in the student as a person, they are in danger of getting involved with his problems and neglecting his "education." In reality, however, many teachers would benefit greatly from a little more "involvement." As they became more interested in what the student is like as a person and how he develops under the impact of the college, they would develop a new view of their own teaching.

V

Links
with the
Larger Society

17

Individual
Development
After or Outside
of College

On commencement day, seniors are told that education for them has only begun, that society expects them to go on learning as college has taught them to do. Of these graduates, many take advantage of professional schools, on-the-job training, or evening courses in adult education, but apart from this learning, how many continue to develop personally instead of just remaining as they were at graduation or even regressing to an earlier stage?

According to personality theory, developmental change can occur at any time of life: each of us, at whatever age, has unexpressed potentialities. What actually happens depends on conditions that can, to some extent, be controlled. A person develops by mastering situations in which none of his former responses will work and new ones must thus be evolved. If a person remains unchallenged, he ceases to develop; and if the challenges are too strange or strong, he may turn away or adapt in harmful ways. In contrast to these extremes, the provision of useful challenges has seldom been the object of scientific study.

When we studied patterns of development at Vassar College, giving personality

tests to entire classes over a period of time, we were struck by the
relatively high level of instability or "upsetness" of the seniors, who
were examined in the spring just before graduation. Shocked out of
their comfortable adjustments to college, they were now focused
upon the outside world, with its unknown demands, and upon the
need to make decisions and commit themselves—often for the first
time—in ways that seemed irreversible. Under this stress, they
seemed to us unusually educable, open to knowledge of the world
and of themselves. Educators at Bowdoin College were so struck by
these observations that they started a whole new plan of general
education for seniors, designed to take advantage of this special openness to learning. In our own further work in undergraduate education, we have asked whether this heightened educability could not
be induced earlier than the senior year.

How is it with alumni, however, five or twenty-five
years after graduation? On the basis of studies in which the same
people were examined as seniors and again four or five years later,
Freedman (1962) found that young alumnae, though less disturbed
or upset than they were as seniors, still had largely the same values
and attitudes; that in the years since graduation, they had become
more stable, but not really developed much further. Their growth
curves had leveled off. Studies of Vassar alumnae of various generations, going back to 1904, strongly suggest that values and attitudes
change during college much more easily than later, and that for
many students college thus offers a kind of "last chance" for serious
development.

Evidence of this leveling off, of sameness over the years,
may seem to contradict what I said about the possibilities of developmental change at any age, but so far I have spoken only of
averages. From studies of individual graduates, we know that some
fall from grace: after leaving college in a spirit of "so much for
education," they soon return to patterns characteristic of them as
freshmen. From statistical inference and studies of other alumnae,
however, we also know that some young people show more development during the four or five years after graduation than most students show during college: just as some seniors look back with a
certain discomfort upon what they were like as freshmen, some

graduates look back after four years, perhaps with amused tolerance, upon their senior selves.

The years immediately following college offer challenges of great potency—the first job, a move to a different environment, marriage, parenthood, and domestic crises of various kinds. These challenges lead to further development, provided one's liberal education has "taken" and enabled him to respond creatively. In contrast, a premature marriage or career choice—say, at age seventeen—may so absorb a person in his role requirements as to prevent him from having the experiences he needs to develop.

In order to understand various growth curves, we need to reconsider the tension in personality between a curiosity about new ideas, people, and skills, and a need to stop and organize the assortment to which our curiosity has already led. In development, each of these processes requires the other, for if either acts alone, the student will suffer prolonged confusion or the opposite fault of premature closure. During college, students repeatedly arrive at vocational choices or philosophies or styles of adult life that have to be given up in the interests of further learning and, in time, of a new integration on a higher level of complexity.

In the years that immediately follow the end of formal education, integration is at a premium: commitments to particular social roles require that the graduate organize himself, use the knowledge he already has, and abandon alternatives which had up to then been seriously considered. The young man often feels that he must establish himself quickly; his wife feels that she must be an even better mother than her own mother was and must acquire, overnight if possible, all the stigmata of middle-class domestic life. In other words, they dig those ruts from which it is later so hard to get out. In the face of such pressures, education beyond college requires the perspective provided by a developmental psychology, a model of growth appropriate not just to a single stage, but to the entire life span.

A longer-term model would emphasize, for example, that a student unsure of what vocation to answer should take the time to experiment with several fields and, in trying his hand, should seek the rewards of risk in place of a premature security. From the same model of development, a recent graduate could learn that if some of his major aspirations are unfulfilled by the work he has chosen, it is not too late to nurture the unorganized, unutilized parts of himself and seek better ways to give them expression. When we studied intensively a group of alumnae at Vassar, 20 to 25 years after graduation, we found that characteristically these women rediscovered in themselves hopes and plans for the future that had existed when they graduated from college but had long been neglected. Stimulated by participation in our study, some of these alumnae launched themselves upon new careers or in new directions of activity.

The problem is that, in our society, conditions for such development are rarely suitable. Intellectual stimulation in the form of classes at night school or on educational television at six in the morning is attached less to the day's concerns than to one end or the other of sleep. Although one's spouse will hopefully serve as an intellectual companion, development during adult life requires support not only in the family but in larger circles of many kinds—in discussion groups, in weekend classes, in summer institutes, even in sabbaticals for businessmen. In promoting these and other arrangements, every institution can play its part, from clubs to corporations.

New forms and wide participation in evolving them are necessary in extending opportunities not only for those who want a continuing education after college but also for young people who now have no chance for higher education at all and who may lack the peculiar skills necessary for success in college as we know it.

Universal Higher Education. In 1947 President Truman's Commission on Higher Education issued a statement of educational purposes that sums up the spirit in which this book is written:

> To liberate and perfect the intrinsic powers of every citizen is the central purpose of democracy; and its furtherance of individual self-realization is its greatest glory. . . . The first goal of education for democracy is the full, rounded, and continuing development of the person.

If we are truly dedicated to the ideal of higher education for individual development, we cannot leave this discussion without giving some consideration to the great number of our young people who do not now go to college. These youngsters, too, will have to cope with an automated, super-organized, and impersonal world; with increased leisure, world citizenship, and many of the other problems that will challenge their college-educated brothers. With only a high school education, and sometimes less than that, they face those problems poorly prepared. Even though many American high schools are doing an excellent job, young people need as much help in the four years after graduation as in those before. In the process of development, some things must be accomplished before others are possible; and at the age of eighteen, for example, much ordinarily remains to be done.

Among young people who now end their education at eighteen or before, some have the ability for college but lack the money; and for them we are extending the range of student loans and scholarships, and establishing new community and junior colleges. On the other hand, the increasing population of adolescents and the steadily rising requirements for college entrance put college education beyond the reach of young persons with modest academic talents, and many others have been so deprived of middle-class culture that they are unable to profit even from existing secondary programs, to say nothing of further academic work. In order to give these disadvantaged students an opportunity to realize whatever level of development they are capable of, we are going to have to design new institutions and new approaches to teaching. It is unimaginable that schools as they are now constituted can do all that needs to be done for these students.

Often, when the issue of character education or education for personal development is discussed in educational circles, we hear the objection that these things should be left to other institutions of our society. For vast numbers of children and young people, however, there are no such institutions, not any more. As we approach the challenge of universal higher education, we need to keep in mind that the poor, the culturally deprived, even the stupid are our own. In the absence of effective institutions for helping them, a society that cares for its own has no alternative to creating new institutions in which the child or young person who has low intelligence or is "unmotivated" can be educated up to the level of his potential, which now is usually unknown. Given our present affluence and our promise for the future, we can take seriously the prospect of realizing what the Truman Commission called democracy's "greatest glory"—the fullest possible development of each individual.

Even after going through his education, however, a person may lack the means for functioning as a totally independent, self-starting, self-determining individual, a sort of entrepreneur who will sell his labor in the most favorable market. Thomas Jefferson was right in saying that we ought to give every person a chance to develop himself as an individual—an opportunity lost in the sort of urban slum that Jefferson warned against so vividly. Until their environment becomes reasonably supportive, our less privileged citizens will either fail to take part in higher education or will learn with difficulty; and even those who do manage to learn will find few ways to put their knowledge to work. For people caught in this condition, we have to go beyond the deceptive slogan of "equal opportunity."

In designing new institutions for universal higher education, we have to take our young people as they are. Since large numbers of them are handicapped by personal limitations or by deprivations in their past, and are thus unable to benefit from existing programs of education, it is our task to create programs and institutions from which they *can* benefit.

One source of new models might well be the Job Corps and other projects created by the Office of Economic Opportunity for young people who have been culturally deprived. The establishment of residential centers for girls sixteen to twenty-one who have grown up in poverty is particularly interesting. These centers, it seems, have to be more than trade schools; they must be institutions for general development. The girls cannot be taught very much in the way of basic skills until their self-conceptions have been changed and they have been induced to orient themselves toward the future. The imagination that is going into the planning of these centers is more sophisticated than what is ordinarily found in contemporary planning for institutions of higher learning. In part, this may be due to the fact that the planners represent many professions in addition to education, and are thus relatively free of the assumptions and habits of thought that entrap many of us who have spent long years in educational institutions.

In one key respect, the new institutions we create must be something like colleges. However much we may also emphasize work or social organization or variety of experience, exercises of a more or less intellectual nature are still the best means for promoting development of the total personality, since development after the initial acquisition of language relies heavily on the use of symbols. Psychological development is largely a matter of expanding the range of symbols that can be appreciated and of responses that can be made—a process that again involves the use of symbols.

It is in the life of the imagination that the individual can express most appropriately, even most joyfully, his impulses and feelings. It is in solving problems with the use of intelligence (typically in the manipulation of symbols) and in being held to the requirement of seeking and being guided by the truth that the individual in time develops the functions that enable him to control himself in accord with the demands of reality. And it is largely through confrontation with a wide range of value systems and ethical dilemmas that conscience becomes enlightened and stabilized. With a suitable education, even the dullest youngster can advance in these ways—as, in a different sense, can the culturally deprived child whose mind has often been unchallenged by school, unappreciated at home, and diverted to the peculiar demands of the culture of poverty.

In order to be effective our new institutions will have to be far more flexible than the college or university as we now know it. For example, students should have easy access in and out so that, sure of admission, they can attend part time or drop out temporarily to work or to have some other kind of experience. Every student who "finished" such an institution would understand that he had to go on learning, and that from time to time he might return to his school to do so. This freedom to combine schooling with another style of life should be available not only to the culturally deprived but to college graduates who develop new interests.

Recently we had some experience with the latter group at the Institute for the Study of Human Problems at Stanford. As part of our work for the Cooperative Commission on the Study of Alcoholism, we enlisted several members of the Junior League of San Francisco. These ladies were members of the League's committee on alcoholism and were enthusiastic at the prospect of serving as research assistants in a study of teen-age drinking. Along with the staff they helped to design the interview schedule, choose a suitable sample, conduct the interviews, and analyze the data.

In my opinion this little experiment was a great success. From the Institute's viewpoint, a worthwhile piece of research was carried out without undue expenditure of staff time, and for the League members, it offered an opportunity to continue their education. Each worker not only learned a great deal about teen-agers, alcohol, and methods of inquiry in social science, but was able to sort out some of her personal attitudes toward her own drinking and that of her children. This introspection was an educational experience in its own right.

The community at large also profits from this kind of collaboration. As soon as intelligent persons acquire a sense of familiarity with the facts about a social problem, they think in quite concrete terms about what should be done. It seemed to us that the young women with whom we worked were on the road to becoming community leaders, and their experience at the Institute helped to make them especially alert to the ordinarily taboo subject of alcohol problems and to the crude and distorted stereotypes of teen-agers so common today. Before our study had been under way long, our socialite-assistants discovered that when the conversation lagged at dinner parties they could bring up the subject of their research; and as they prepared for community action on these problems, the members of the Junior League were in a position to enlist not only their own resources but those of their husbands. It would not be difficult to develop such groups on a large scale, and we may imagine a time when faculty members of educational centers spend relatively little of their time in classroom teaching and most of their time generating ideas and organizing activities in which people of different ages and different walks of life educate each other.

The final question is, "*Who* is going to meet the challenges of universal higher education, especially the design and staffing of new types of institutions?" I am afraid that college faculties are not likely to be very much interested in the problem. Our graduate schools have not put in their curricula any courses or professional programs designed to prepare people to run institutions of the kind we need. Most psychologists and other academicians or researchers specialize in narrower areas of knowledge rather than dealing with such large problems as how people develop and how they might develop better. One might think that teachers in the community colleges would be good candidates for work in this field, but the goal of many of them is to be like professors in prestige institutions.

To staff our new institutions permanently, I believe that we must develop a new profession, a profession in which generally educated people become specialists in individual development and in the operation of institutions designed for this purpose. In the meanwhile we might use not only the persons who are now engaged in counseling on student affairs in our best universities and colleges, but also those who are now doing individual psychotherapy, a form of treatment apparently declining in popularity. Some returning Peace Corpsmen might also be well suited to this work; several thousand return to the country each year with experience that is probably excellent preparation for what we have in mind. And of course we should recruit teachers from community colleges who really want to teach students instead of merely becoming researchers.

Those who are willing to commit themselves to the service of universal higher education will find unparalleled opportunities for experimentation, both in the design of new kinds of institutions and in the trying out of various approaches in them. If such experimentation is not to be hit or miss, it must be guided by theory and by more knowledge than we now have about how people in the relevant age range may develop, about what kinds of changes in what areas of the person may now be induced, and through what kinds of experiences. Much could be learned from careful observation of what happens as the result of different institutional programs, but it is not to be expected that this experimentation can proceed according to the model usually employed in laboratory research. People who undertake new educational ventures rarely do so merely out of curiosity; they have a passionate concern with what they are doing and faith in its effectiveness. Thus the question of "what works better" will have to be answered by researchers who have the opportunity to observe two or more institutions or practices at the same time with due attention to necessary "controls." As a research project, this type of experiment is hard to carry out and rarely yields satisfactory answers; but as a venture in social change, it succeeds simply by helping the students and by thus attracting support from the community; and in the case of success, it persists far beyond the time when we would call it an experiment. Another index of the success of such an enterprise would be the degree to which it influenced, or became a model for, other colleges. Interestingly enough, these successes may become apparent before the results of any scientific evaluation become available.

It follows that the benefits of educational experimentation may lie not so much in what can be found out as in the effects that the experiment has upon those who take part in it. An educational experiment almost always interests and challenges the students who are its objects. Thus it is that the processes which make scientific work in this field extraordinarily difficult are the very ones that lead to immediate educational gains.

If we use sound personality theory as our guide in experimenting with new institutions for the least privileged of our young people, I would not be surprised to find that in time most citizens would demand the same kind of opportunity for *their* children. This was the experience of boarding schools in the Soviet Union. Planned at first for children who for one reason or another could not live at home, these schools were so attractive and successful that soon the elite of the country were demanding that their children be admitted, as indeed they were. I am sure that many a parent, on observing the work that Martin Deutsch and his group are doing for poor children in New York, would wish that his own youngsters could have something as good.

Not all of the culturally deprived are to be found among school dropouts; they may also be found among people in college and even among those who have managed to graduate. Not infrequently these individuals are encountered in mental-hygiene clinics and psychiatric hospitals. Recently I heard the case of a young woman who suffered from a morbid fear of eating in public places. It was possible without much difficulty to formulate her case in psychoanalytic terms, but, as the history unfolded, it became clear that probably her greatest problem was a lack of those resources that we ordinarily expect to come from education. Although she had come from a home which, in purely economic terms, would have to be described as upper-middle-class, and had gone to college for a year, she had never learned to read with enjoyment or to do anything that might enhance self-respect or offer self-fulfillment. Her personality seemed to have been formed through watching television and reading advertisements which instructed her in how to be "feminine," in the narrowest sense of that word. Now the wife of an airman and living on a base, she had no notion of what to do with herself. Probably having a baby would help her, but then one would worry about the future of the baby. Psychotherapy would no doubt remove her major symptom, but she could be given the full course of psychotherapy without alteration in the principal cause of her difficulty: she would still have to be educated. Indeed, it can be argued that if she *were* properly educated—starting now, when she is twenty-two—she would probably not need psychotherapy.

Supporting this general point was the experience that some of us had when working in a county mental-hygiene clinic. Among the patients were wives of Ph.D.s who worked at the local electronics laboratory. These young women, who typically had dropped out of college to get married and who had two or three children, brought us all kinds of interesting "symptoms"; but it dawned on us in time that their real trouble was the lack of someone to talk with. Usually it was the husbands who had been culturally deprived. All they could talk about was "shop" and sports; their education had neglected the areas of humane feeling, and their boredom and insensitivity when it came to such questions as what might be a good life for the children left their wives in despair. There was not much that we could do.

Our large state mental institutions have been filled with

people for whom life in our complex society has become too difficult.
A generation ago, most of them would have led more or less un-
troubled lives working at simple jobs in human communities. Today
they display a wide range of psychiatric symptoms. What many of
them have in common is a kind of incompetence; the skills they may
have learned have become valueless, and they lack the resources for
coping with the ordinary demands of life. To supply the necessary
resources will require new forms of education both for those who
find no place in college and for graduates who missed crucial stages
of personal development.

No matter how successful the new programs of universal
higher education might be, they would not be a threat to institutions
that now devote themselves to specialized excellence, building strong
departments and preparing many students for graduate school.
When the new institutions became known for their good teaching,
however, they might attract young people of the kind who now enter
colleges, and their success would hasten the day when our colleges
and universities devote themselves more fully to the ideal of developing the full human potential of every student.

18

General Education and the Human Problems Institute

Our society needs not only creative scientists but also people who can recognize and appreciate them, create conditions favorable to their work, and make judgments about what they might do. It needs people who can make contributions in various fields of human endeavor, people who at various levels of talent and responsibility can be useful in our complex and troubled society.

Education to produce good scientists and good men—that is to say, education aimed at developing the individual's potential as fully as possible—is in the best sense *general education*. Introducing the student to a range of subjects and ideas, as in survey courses— sometimes called general education—is *not* the essential thing, though this may be a useful instrument of general education. Developing the generalist approach to inquiry, the synthetic function, is closer to the mark; and so is involvement in significant experiences with people and things. But this is by no means all. General education aims at development toward full humanity, and all the resources of a college should be organized to this end.

Among the resources of a college, clearly the teacher

is central. Whatever curricular reforms may be instituted, whatever changes in the organization of teaching or in the social life of the college may be made, whatever schemes might be concocted or gadgets contrived, nothing very good can happen unless there are teachers with some enthusiasm for educating the undergraduate. This need for effective teachers is a cause of great dismay among those who feel responsibility and concern for American higher education. The Carnegie Foundation (1964) reports grimly that there is no significant increase in the proportion of new Ph.D.s going into college or university work (45.2 per cent in 1954–55, 46.7 per cent in 1961–62) to meet the dramatic increase in the proportion of young people who are entering college. But this is only part of the problem. In addition, as federal expenditures for research and development increase (over two hundred times between 1940 and 1964), faculty members of our colleges and universities do less and less teaching. And most serious of all from the point of view of one interested in education for individual development, much of the teaching that is currently done is specialized and preprofessional and thus not well-calculated to induce developmental changes in students.

Declining interest in teaching undergraduates is part of a larger picture of decline of the liberal college. This has been eloquently lamented by numerous university leaders, such as Barzun (1964), Brown (1964), and DeVane (1964). It has been shrewdly but less passionately analyzed by Kerr (1964). According to these writers, the college is being "squeezed" between the high school and the graduate school; the former is tending to do what the first two years of college used to do while the latter is extending its ways of doing things onto the last two years of college. Owing mainly to the prestige and power of the graduate schools, which are increasingly specialized and endowed with research funds, there is great pressure upon the university man to define himself as more specialist than intellectual, more researcher than teacher, more a teacher of graduate students than of undergraduates. Knapp (1962) has supplied documentation for this point; and to the college or university man of today this state of affairs seems as real as the new freeway through his district.

The kind of specialization of which we have been

speaking is embodied in its purest form in the research professor working on the frontiers of knowledge with advanced graduate students and postdoctoral scholars. He provides the ideal for the rest of the faculty, who fight for appointments that will come as close to his as possible. The undergraduate is left out—not only because the faculty's interest is elsewhere but also because the specializations of knowledge and professional language require a long, dull period of mastery before the student can share the professor's concerns.

Specialization has even deeper implications for the student; it contributes toward the fragmentation of *him*. When everything in nature is conceived as being susceptible to abstraction for purposes of intensive study, the student himself does not escape: he too is conceived as an aggregate of such part-processes as intelligence, sex, creativity, motivation—each of which can be studied separately from the rest and each of which is to be dealt with by special machinery set up for that purpose. If a teacher has this conception of the student, it is easy for him to say that he is interested only in the student's intellect, which is categorically separated from the rest of him. Or it may be the other way around: if one insists that education is only a matter of transferring specialized knowledge and skills to the student, then the student comes to be conceived as the embodiment of bits of knowledge and particular skills. With no instruction on the integration of the knowledge he acquires, the student—unless he rebels—begins to live according to the prevailing conception of him and eventually identifies himself with the system. Thus the students, both successful and unsuccessful, become reflections of the system in which they live for four years.

The problem is how to enlarge college and university faculties and how to persuade more of their members to take an interest in general education. It is usually supposed that this can be done either by love or by money.

The love is there, but it is inhibited. An academic man who takes an interest in his students as developing individuals will be regarded by his colleagues as weak, or neurotic, or—what is worse—anti-intellectual. Even so, many teachers are responsive to the call of students for some attention; often they initiate arrangements for improving faculty-student relations or for offering students something fresh and interesting. But initial enthusiasm soon fades, and the project is abandoned. Incentives are not sufficiently real or enduring.

Money seems at first glance more promising. But the big money goes for research; and even if substantial sums were poured into undergraduate teaching, it would be filtered through the existing university apparatus, with the great likelihood that most of it would wind up in the budgets of departments eager to install new courses at the frontiers of their disciplines.

Need for Reorganization in the Search for Knowledge. The educational problem is deeply imbedded in social dynamics, and efforts at reform must be directed to the real seat of the trouble: the way in which the search for knowledge is organized and the effects of this structure upon both society and education. I will argue that specialization in inquiry and in teaching, while necessary, has led through its very success to the creation of new problems—to a serious neglect of the generalist approach, as well as to a misconception, even abuse, of the student. Then I will propose that a solution to our current dilemma requires the restoration of the generalizing and synthesizing function to its proper place in science and that such a restoration would encourage a style of teaching that recognizes and nourishes the humanity of the student.

The potentiality for creating fresh human problems is inherent in the dynamics of specialized knowledge, whose sudden thrusts within a limited sector of a social system creates imbalances in the whole. For example, the great effectiveness of specialized scientific inquiry is evident in the success of medical science in reducing rates of mortality. But the resulting "population explosion" has had to develop to the point of imminent world catastrophe before the need for a proportionate reallocation of resources to the resulting problem could be seen as a matter for serious scientific attention. The long delay between the creation of such knowledge-consequent problems and the slow, cumbersome organization of the means to meet them often spells human tragedy on a large scale. The apparatus originally set up for coping with particular problems develops self-perpetuating mechanisms and continues to operate along the same lines as before. Thus the university structure of departments, schools, and research institutes is exceedingly difficult to change, even though the problems they help to create do not fall within the domain of any one of them nor lend themselves to attack by their favored methods.

New problems, or old problems that have been neglected because they do not fit into existing apparatus, have to be approached in the first instance with the use of generalist methods, the neglect of which is at the heart of both our human and our educational problems. A generalist approach requires, first, a recognition that problems that arise as a result of social changes constitute new ranges of empirical phenomena. They are not at the frontier of any science, even though they may be in the forefront of the ordinary citizen's attention. They cannot be attacked with the most advanced methods or the most sophisticated concepts of existing disciplines; instead they call for exploratory or qualitative study, which is directed to their proper definition, to the understanding of their connections with other problems, and to the generation of new concepts and methods.

A generalist approach also interprets inquiry to mean not only the discovery or demonstration of facts but also the organization and interpretation of them. If knowledge is to serve human purposes, if it is to develop into wisdom, facts from various fields of specialized inquiry have to be brought together and evaluated in relation to the new problems that emerge as a consequence of applications of specialized research. Such continually new organizations of knowledge require a capacity to draw from several existing fields cutting across the departmental divisions that have grown up around advanced specialties. If this is not done, we shall continue to be faced with enormous human and social problems despite an "explosion in knowledge"—which is, in effect, a proliferation of facts and a *contraction* of understanding.

It is proposed that universities and colleges set up multidisciplinary institutes for the study of pressing human problems. Such an addition to existing departments would radically alter the relation of a proportion of our scholars to their field of inquiry and to their undergraduate students. It would also leave departments to continue what they do best: the advanced education of the professional specialist.

The Human Problems Institute at Stanford. An example of what is proposed—a preliminary model—is the Institute for the Study of Human Problems at Stanford University. This Institute was started in 1961 with two research grants, one for studying and making policy recommendations about alcohol problems, the other for studying how college students develop as individuals and how they might be induced to develop more fully. The staff of the Institute embraced at least one person trained in each of the following fields: Psychology, Sociology, Anthropology, Political Science, Social Welfare, Psychiatry, Education, Law, Literature, Public Health, Philosophy, and Bio-Statistics. This group has worked closely together for four years and most have experienced a gradual loosening of their original disciplinary ties. Although the Institute began without any plans for teaching (beyond providing places for research assistants), and although most of the staff have been full-time researchers, it is significant that most have been drawn into undergraduate teaching. This teaching has been mainly informal or somewhat special; for example, members of the staff have led senior colloquia, supervised independent reading and research, and taught courses in higher education for selected student leaders. All members of the staff, including young men and women who have yet to establish themselves in their careers, have said they would be happy to teach in an undergraduate general studies program while doing the same kind of research—provided that the program was new, interesting, and well-conceived and that there was reasonable job security.

Another example is the Center for Research on Conflict Resolution at the University of Michigan, where multidisciplinary research and the training of graduate students have proliferated into undergraduate teaching.

A Model Human-Problems Institute. In the remainder of this chapter I would like to suggest what might be the ideal role of the human-problems institute—something of how such an institute might operate and what might be its best role in teaching. On the basis of our experience at Stanford I will, at the same time, indicate some of the problems and some of the promises of such an institute.

Problems might be selected according to four main criteria: whether the problem is of deep human concern, whether it requires for its solution the resources of several disciplines, whether it is being neglected by those who have the capacity to solve it, and whether it is possible to get financial support for work on it.

Problems related to the use of alcohol in our society qualify according to these criteria. Alcoholism is a major health problem and it ranks high among the problems dealt with by a variety of welfare and law enforcement agencies. According to present indications, the alcoholic condition is a result of an interplay of biological, psychological, and social factors; an understanding of it will be attained only through the close collaboration of researchers from several disciplines. Partly because of the complexity of the problem, it has been badly neglected. There are various reasons for the unpopularity of alcoholism as a phenomenon to study or to treat; but, because it has many facets and can be viewed in different perspectives, it has been easy for university departments and schools and various professional groups to pass it along to someone else. Yet, from the point of view of policy-makers at high levels of government, the problem is so serious that ample funds for research are available—far more, in fact, than can be allocated.

The study of individual development in college also meets the four criteria listed above. Although the development of young people is the main, though often unexpressed, concern of parents who send their sons and daughters to college, and although knowledge of how students change under the influence of educational procedures must be the basis for educational policy, this whole area has been neglected by psychologists and educational researchers because it does not lend itself to investigation by the more specialized methods of these disciplines. The field has in recent years begun to receive some attention from researchers; and now that students have at last found their voices, there is hope that a major effort will be made to understand their experiences and needs and how they might best be educated.

There is no lack of problems: war and peace, economic

planning, the improved working of democratic institutions, race relations, poverty, rehabilitation of the culturally deprived, the deterioration of our cities, the swelling population, the alienation and demoralization of youth, aging and longevity, air pollution and other environmental hazards to health, addictions of various kinds, conservation and land use, and so on. Problems in any one of these areas might well be made the focus of study in a multidisciplinary institute. These problems are highly salient today and funds are being poured into efforts to solve some of them. It is almost universally assumed, however, that the existing structure of professions and university departments and schools will be adequate to these challenges. Yet when one considers the rapidity of change in our time, this structure seems to have been designed for a different age. One is forced to conclude that there should be institutes for the study of universities.

There are highly important scientific reasons why the institute should work on several problems at the same time. It is just this kind of exposure to differing problems—and the accompanying association with colleagues from different disciplines—that serves to educate the staff in the generalist orientation. Little would be gained if a scientist gave up a disciplinary specialty only to become a specialist in some particular applied area. Work on different problems at the same time would also lead the staff to look for underlying affinities among them—for processes central to a diversity of surface phenomena—and then to make advances on the conceptual and theoretical front.

From the beginning of our work at Stanford we considered it very important that research on alcohol-related problems go forward in a setting that favored close association between the staff of the alcohol project and the staffs of other projects. This was partly to combat the tendency to make of "alcohology" a specialty that could be kept out of the main stream of science and practice, with the consequent development of outgroup attitudes among the "alcohologists" and partly to lend status to what has been a low status field. We wanted to insure that alcohol problems were viewed in new perspectives and that the empirical phenomena of the field were connected with those of other fields.

Other projects have been taken up at our institute since the beginning of the alcohol and student-development studies. A study of institutions for the blind was added because it seemed that it would aid our understanding of agencies that care for, or "cope with," people who have been labeled alcoholics. In the same ways, a study of young people who do not go to college seemed an obvious counterpart to the study of student development, and an epidemiological study of drug use seemed a natural extension of our investigations of alcohol use. The major considerations in adding a project have been that the person who wanted to do it shared the values and research ideology of the then-existing staff and that there was a good likelihood that it would benefit and be benefited by existing projects.

The fact that people of different disciplines work under the same roof and have the same general research interests and ideology does not mean that their collaboration will be very close. The pull of the specialty is strong. For close collaboration across disciplines the shared problem is the thing. If a group of scholars and scientists are required to make recommendations for action with respect to an important problem, and if they stay together at all, there is a strong tendency for them to pull together.

For example: Should the age at which young people are permitted by law to purchase or possess alcoholic beverages in public places be held at twenty-one, as usual, should it be lowered to eighteen, or should it be dispensed with altogether? Our "alcohol staff" has the obligation to work out a defensible position on this question. It seems that in order to do so we need a great deal of knowledge about the nature and determinants of different patterns of drinking among young people and about the implications of particular patterns for the later development of the individual. To act in the interest of young people we have to know them rather well—as personalities in a stage of development, and in respect to their situation in our society today. For to be reasonably sure that an action affecting people does not do more harm than good, it is necessary to consider possible consequences for various areas of their lives. This is true for the individual, and it is also true for the social group. A change in the drinking laws, for example, would amount to a change in our

culture. Various groups and institutions in our society have a strong
interest in the matter; and any judgment of the feasibility of such a
change would have to be based on an appraisal of the climate of
opinion in these groups and institutions, as well as in the population
generally.

To organize knowledge around problems of this kind, to
confront the various issues of value that are involved, and to lay
plans for studying the consequences of actions—all require the
closest interdisciplinary collaboration. In our experience, the representatives of the various disciplines mentioned above have been fully
challenged, and we have felt the need to draw upon other disciplines
as well. When scholars and scientists work on problems of this kind,
they become highly stimulated and communication becomes very
free and is carried on without benefit of specialized terminology. Each
member of the group is grateful for the contributions of various
disciplines and he becomes appropriately realistic about what his
own has to offer.

The same kind of close collaboration has been attained
by the psychologists, psychiatrists, social workers, and educators who
are studying student development with attention to educational
policy. But the same circumstances that led to maximum cross-
disciplinary fertilization and intellectual companionship among the
alcohol and the student-development staffs tended at the same time
to draw the two groups apart—even though the two staffs over-
lapped to some extent. This is testimony both to the power of the
shared problem to pull people together and to the difficulty of researchers becoming generalists when they work on sponsored projects
that entail pressure to meet deadlines. Even so, the alcohol and
student-development projects have interpenetrated one another in
fruitful ways. The study of students has contributed directly to our
knowledge of drinking among youth, and the study of drinking patterns and liquor-control policies on the campus—in important ways
a microcosm of the larger society—has aided our efforts to help
formulate general policy. At the same time it has been discovered
that a student's approach to alcohol and his relations with drinking
subcultures are very significant expressions of his personality and the
developmental changes within it.

To accent social need is not to say that the problem-centered institute represents "applied science" in the ordinary sense of this term. There are, of course, institutes of applied science deliberately organized and staffed by "practical" men who try to exploit knowledge created by university departments and research institutes. To some extent the human-problems institute participates in this kind of applied work, but the study of new problems that arise as a result of social change broadens the empirical base of the component sciences upon which the institute draws and leads to the creation of new concepts. A well-constructed idea always has a definite relation to the empirical events that it seeks to conceptualize. If the observational base is narrow, the concept can have little generality. An observer who studies his subjects in an extended environment, as the problem-oriented researcher must usually do, will invent different concepts than will an observer who confines himself to laboratory or clinical situations. Thus, in a clinical situation, the therapist-theorist who usually works with adults who are still caught up in continuing childhood conflicts would not see that considerable change in personality takes place during the college years—a finding that resulted from our study of college students. This finding has resulted in new concepts for dealing with the conditions and processes of change at later stages.

Psychology of the sort that is taught in basic courses and that is central to most of the research that is published in the journals consists mainly of concepts that have relatively narrow empirical bases. Yet there is a great public expectation that psychology will somehow supply answers to various kinds of pressing practical problems. This has led to a tendency to bring to the complex phenomena of real life concepts that are almost ludicrously inappropriate, as when it is supposed that a psychology of learning derived from laboratory studies can be applied directly to education for individual development at the college level. In the absence of empirical information about how students actually learn and of models derived from realistic observations, the tendency is to apply models from the laboratory and, when they do not fit, to try to make life itself conform to the laboratory.

To be practical, the psychologist and social scientist

must deal with long sections of behavior and with large areas of the person and of the social system. They must also do this in order to be good scientists. The processes of nature are not first of all isolated objects of inquiry waiting to be observed and then synthesized; they exist, instead, in contexts of other processes and can be fully understood only when seen in their natural setting. Although inquiry proceeds by analysis and by the intensive study of part-processes that have been abstracted from the wholes in which they are naturally embedded, the wholes must be reconstituted if they and their parts are to be known well.

It seems then, that knowledge of how things fit together is at least as important in science as is knowledge of how things may be analyzed. This is freely admitted by most scientists, but the objecton can be raised that complex wholes and wide ranges of variables cannot be studied by existing scientific methods. The answer is that we *must,* sooner or later, study complex and wide-ranging phenomena if our sciences are ever to become fully developed. My suggestion is that one way to be holistic, comprehensive, and generalist in one's approach is to be practical.

This is a key conception in the human-problems approach. In thinking comprehensively and holistically about human or social problems, the scientist must use gross units of analysis, and he must content himself with rough estimates of the variables he studies. He cannot hope soon to achieve the refinement of conceptualization and the precision of measurement that is achieved by the laboratory man, but this does not make him any the less scientific—not if he makes certain that his gross categories are not inconsistent with what is known at lower levels and that they lend themselves to reduction and systematic treatment.

There is another way in which the human-problems approach should be distinguished from applied science: in the former the scientist does not accept the surface definition of the problem; instead, the definition of the problem becomes a part of his inquiry. When he is called upon by individuals or groups to help solve a problem it almost always turns out that they have a narrow view of what the trouble is and an unrealistic conception of what they want to accomplish. The scientist cannot be content to bring his expertise to bear on such problems as how to keep school children quiet, how to forestall civil-rights demonstrations, or how to prevent eighteen-year-olds from drinking. This would be unscientific, as well as unhelpful to those who sought counsel. When a scientist concerns himself with matters such as these the most useful thing he can do is to help define the problem and to bring about a fresh consideration of goals. By starting with the assumption that practical problems are complex, interwoven with other problems, and tied to long-range human and social goals, the scientist initiates a process of inquiry in which his clients become involved and in the course of which he may ask questions of general scientific interest. Often the question will take the form of how might individuals or social structures be changed in some desired way. The phenomena with which the scientist has to deal in working on a particular problem can almost always be regarded as a special case of something more general, and thus he has an opportunity to contribute to systematic knowledge while aiding in the solution of practical problems.

To be immersed fully in the realities of a problem situation—to be engaged with it and concerned to bring about some desirable change—is to be in a situation that is very favorable to the creation of ideas. It is a significant fact that the most seminal concepts for the understanding of the individual personality have been produced by men who were engaged in the practice of psychotherapy. The development of a social therapy which aimed to overcome failings of social systems could be equally productive of ideas for the understanding of social processes. The individual scientist who engaged in this activity would be fully challenged; he would be concerned as well as curious; and this would favor his success. He might at some times, when the demonstration of hypotheses was the order of the day, allow a part of his scientific conscience to dominate his work; but for the most part he could function as a whole human being, whose nature it is to inquire.

The idea of a multidisciplinary institute devoted to current human or social problems is not new. The Yale Institute of Human Relations and the several institutes of child welfare established in the 1930s had this general purpose. But history records a strong tendency for such institutes to transform themselves into

centers for specialized sciences. It has proved to be very easy for
faculty to work in these centers without surrendering any of their
disciplinary concerns or professional identity. And departments, it
seems, have always known how to utilize such institutes for their
own purposes, such as bringing in a new man without having to use
departmental funds. The institutes being discussed here cannot be
creatures of the departments.

The usual research center or laboratory is even more
specialized than the university department and therefore differs from
the human-problems institute. Problems are chosen for their direct
relevance to the development of some aspect of a science, and the
professional constraints upon staff members are as great as they are
in departments. This is true even though several such centers or
laboratories or projects are, for administrative purposes, brought together in the same "institute"; and it may be true even though staff
members are drawn from several departments. Institutes or centers
for the study of "learning" or of "cognitive processes" are concerned
with problems at the frontiers of psychology and are highly specialized, even though staff members may come from Philosophy,
Mathematics, Education, Sociology, Speech or Communication, as
well as from Psychology. It is to the work of such centers that we
owe some of those advances in knowledge that help to upset the
existing equilibrium and make human-problems institutes necessary.

Finally, the human-problems institute is different from
all those centers where scholars and scientists of different disciplines
come together just to exchange and generate ideas. The kind of
institute being advocated here is multidisciplinary because the problems with which it is concerned can be attacked only in this way.
And in such an institute all staff members engage in research, though
they need not, and preferably do not, do so exclusively.

The Institute's Potential Role in Teaching. Today,
when there is a great deal of discussion of innovations in general
education, and when experimental programs are actually being set
in motion, it is almost universally assumed that teachers will be
borrowed from their departments for a while or that they will be
allowed to keep one foot in their departments while giving themselves wholeheartedly to a new venture. The setting up of problem-

centered institutes can help to sustain educational innovations, for a new and challenging general education program is a natural base for the teaching activities of the generalist researcher. More than this, if staff members of problem-centered institutes were affiliated with undergraduate teaching programs, this would help to maintain the stability of these institutes. It may be added also that college teachers who do not have adequate opportunities for research might well organize, or have organized for them, multidisciplinary institutes of the sort being advocated here.

The problem-oriented generalist may be or may become uniquely qualified for a particular kind of undergraduate teaching, especially valuable to the undergraduate. The researcher on human problems has to proceed in an exploratory way, and he cannot rely on the technical terms of his parent discipline. He is not, therefore, in a very good position to talk to graduate students, who are likely to feel that they know everything already, or even to those undergraduates who know exactly what they want to do and are in a hurry to envelop themselves in the cloak of a specialty. But the open-ended, curious undergraduate is a natural audience and companion; and men who are engaged, as men and as scientists, with pressing problems about which little is known and who are generating ideas *do* need an audience.

The entering freshman is a natural generalist. Often he thinks that a college professor can talk on any subject; and, in his questioning, he leaps from topic to topic, although they are somehow related in his mind. It is only later, probably just a few weeks later, that he discovers that different questions have to be asked of different people and that he himself must learn to keep his knowledge in separate compartments if he is to be a success in college. How may the freshman's generalist tendencies be nourished? A minimum strategy, surely, is to expose him to a range of subjects. Teaching based in a problem-oriented institute would do this. And since the various problems with which the institute was engaged would be at a relatively early stage of development, the student could be returned to a situation not unlike that of Newton's day, when an educated man could learn all there was to know in several directions.

Still, generalism is not primarily a matter of breadth.

It is inconceivable today that a scholar can have any adequate grasp of all knowledge. Generalism, most essentially, is a form of inquiry and a set of attitudes toward knowledge. The generalist accents the synthetic function; he is out to connect things that have been isolated; but most of all he is impressed by the complexity of things, and he seeks to understand them in their context. There are many ways in which things are related and brought together intellectually. And a fundamentally important sort of cohesion of diverse factors is that which is exposed by the human-problems type of inquiry. It is this that should be put across to students, in the interest of their general education.

It follows from this that students may best come by a generalist orientation in the same way that the mature scholar does, and that is through direct involvement with human and social problems. Institute-based teaching would bring directly to the student some of the phenomena of life, in all their complexity and immediacy; and the work of conceptualization would go on, as it were, before his eyes. The institute could help to provide, in fact, the functional equivalent of the physical scientist's laboratory. Students could take part in some of the institute's field studies and integrate their experiences with their didactic work. More than that, students could find in the institute's teaching program an intellectual and theoretical context for the field work that they do in the normal course of events. They would then discover that which never becomes clear to many college students: that liberal education need not be divorced from life.

There are questions about the place of this kind of experience in the overall undergraduate education of the student. For example, how much of it, and when? One proposal would be that the student take course work in each of several problem areas, these courses substituting for that part of his studies that would normally meet the requirements of a departmental major. Also, if the entering freshman were introduced to the human-problems orientation, it might influence in a favorable way the remainder of his college career; the experience might involve him and win him to the educational enterprise in a way that introductory courses in special fields often do not. He would be offered some protection against premature commitment to a vocation, and some insulation against all the forces of specialized inquiry that he will encounter later.

We supposed in the beginning that whereas under-graduates and post-doctoral students might very well spend some time in our Institute and receive instruction at the hands of our staff, it would not be in general a very good place for graduate students. Under pressure to meet the requirements of their specialized training programs and eager to establish their professional identities, grad-uate students would be impatient with our generalist orientation and would not find within our policy science and long-range studies suitable topics for Ph.D. dissertations.

We had some research assistantships to offer, however; and since 1961, twenty-three graduate students have worked at the Institute. It seems that we had overestimated the problems and dangers. These students now say that they have enjoyed and bene-fited from their Institute experience, particularly from being mem-bers of a relatively small community or household without being handicapped in their pursuit of the degree. At the end of 1966, four of these students have had their Ph.D. theses signed by mem-bers of the Institute staff.

We have changed our minds about graduate educa-tion—and not only because of our experience with students at the Institute. We have been increasingly impressed by the nation's need for psychologically sensitive social scientists who have the basic in-tellectual tools for action-oriented inquiry, and we have become increasingly acquainted with the job opportunities for people of this kind. Most important of all, we believe that we have acquired some understanding of graduate students in general. A great many of them in this age of the Peace Corps are very unhappy with the con-straints of their professional training and with the prospects that lie before them. They would gladly add two years to their period of training and invite an uncertain future in order to feel human again and in order to be able to work on really important problems.

Perhaps in an ideal arrangement, graduate students who worked at a human-problems institute would take part in the teaching of undergraduates who enrolled in the field-oriented courses organized by staff members. These graduate students would be helped to realize that it is undergraduate teaching that holds the university together, that generalist teaching is the best expression of their membership in the university community, and that they have an important role as makers of undergraduate culture.

Conclusion. The existing pattern of undergraduate education in America cannot be changed, fundamentally or enduringly, without reform in our graduate schools, which influence so strongly what is done in the colleges. The great need is for change in the way the search for knowledge is organized. Under present arrangements the college or university teacher is virtually forced to be a specialist, both in his teaching and in research, and he is offered few if any rewards for generalist teaching, which is what the undergraduate needs most. By promoting research directed at human problems, the institute would encourage scholars able to integrate their research and their teaching in general education programs. An institute choosing problems primarily because of their human significance and working on more than one problem at a time would represent a change in existing arrangements: something more than merely a way for paying lip service to the idea of multidisciplinary collaboration, more than a research center for "applied science" of the usual sort. Instead, it would be devoted to pure research of a particular kind. As such, the institute is compatible with existing university structures and the major agencies that support research—a system difficult to support directly.

If one is seriously bent on change the wisest course is to secure funds for other purposes, and to make of change-inducing activities an additional enterprise while faithfully achieving stated purposes. It may thus be possible to initiate change on the fringes of the structure, with some hope of a deeper penetration later. But one would not hope for lasting change unless the innovation was in line with developing social forces. Here there is ground for optimism today. Universities and funding agencies do change—if almost never according to plan. They adapted themselves to the requirements of the Cold War, and they move according to the demands of a technology that nobody controls. They are beginning now to respond to public demands for attention to some of the vast human and social problems that have been created, including that of how to get better teaching, and to an increasingly widely felt desire to break loose from the bonds of technology. This last is expressed in the attitudes and longings of the students—graduate and undergraduate—who come out of the society and into the university. To know these students well is to realize that the period of over-accent on specialization and abandonment to technology is nearing an end. There are many indications that the best students of the present generation, unlike those of the generation that now mans the establishment, want to be educators and social reformers. They want to nourish their humanity and that of others. The conflict of the generations is, in fact, a powerful force toward change. We of the Stanford Institute for the Study of Human Problems believe that, for once, we have correctly anticipated the course of events; we hope to do something that will help shape it to human ends. We do not advocate any radical reduction in specialized inquiry, but only its removal from a position of domination over all of higher education. Problem-oriented institutes would not by themselves accomplish this objective, but they could be the beginning of an effective counterforce.

Bibliography

Academic Senate of the University of California, Berkeley. *Education at Berkeley: Report of the select committee on education.* Berkeley: University of California Academic Senate, 1966.

ALPERT, R., COHEN, S., & SCHILLER, L. *LSD.* New York: New American Library, 1966.

ANDERSON, H. H. Domination and social integration in the behavior of kindergarten children and teachers. *Genetic Psychology Monographs,* 1939, *21,* 287–325.

ANTHONY, R. (pseud.) *The housewife's handbook on selective promiscuity.* New York: Documentary Books, 1962.

ASTIN, A. W. Undergraduate institutions and the production of scientists. *Science,* 1963, *141,* 334–338.

BARRON, F. *Creativity and psychological health: Origins of personal vitality and creative freedom.* Princeton: Van Nostrand, 1963.

BARZUN, J. College to University—and after. *The American Scholar,* 1964, *33,* 212–219.

BEARDSLEE, D., & O'DOWD, D. Students and the occupational world. In N. Sanford (Ed.), *The American col-*

lege. New York: Wiley, 1962.

BEREITER, C., & FREEDMAN, M. B. Fields of study and the people in them. In N. Sanford (Ed.), *The American college.* New York: Wiley, 1962.

BROWN, D. Personality, college environments, and academic productivity. In N. Sanford (Ed.), *The American college.* New York: Wiley, 1962.

BROWN, J. D. The squeeze on the liberal university. *The Atlantic Monthly,* 1964, *213,* 84–87.

BUSHNELL, J. H. Student culture at Vassar. In N. Sanford (Ed.), *The American college.* New York: Wiley, 1962.

Carnegie Foundation for the Advancement of Teaching. *The flight from teaching.* New York, 1964.

CLAY, MARGARET L. Macomb County tackles alcohol education. *The Michigan Alcohol Education Journal,* 1964, *1,* 25–33.

COLEMAN, J. S. Academic achievement and the structure of competition. *Harvard Education Review,* 1959, *29,* 330–351.

CRUTCHFIELD, R. S. Independent thought in a conformist world. In S. Farber & R. H. L. Wilson (Eds.), *Conflict and creativity.* New York: McGraw-Hill, 1963.

DE VANE, W. C. The college of liberal arts. *Daedalus, Fall,* 1964, 1033–1050.

DRESSEL, P. L., & MAYHEW, L. B. *General education: Explorations in evaluation.* Washington, D.C.: American Council on Education, 1954.

ENRIGHT, D. J. Devaluations. *New York Review of Books,* Sept. 8, 1966.

ERIKSON, E. H. *Childhood and society.* New York: Norton, 1955.

FADIMAN, J. Behavior changes following LSD therapy, Doctoral dissertation, Stanford University, 1964.

FALLDING, H. The source and burden of civilization illustrated in the use of alcohol. *Quarterly Journal of Studies on Alcohol,* 1964, *25,* 714–724.

FREEDMAN, M. B. The passage through college. In N. Sanford (Ed.), Personality development during the college years. *Journal of Social Issues,* 1956, *12,* 13–28.

FREEDMAN, M. B. Studies of college alumni. In N. Sanford (Ed.), *The American college.* New York: Wiley, 1962.

FREEDMAN, M. B. The sexual behavior of American college women. *Merrill-Palmer Quarterly,* 1965, *11,* 33–48.

FREEDMAN, M. B., & KANZER, P. Report on the San Mateo youth study. Stanford, California: Institute for the Study of Human Problems, 1966. (Mimeographed.)

FREEDMAN, M. B. *The college experience.* San Francisco: Jossey-Bass, 1967.

GIANNINI, V. Nurturance of talents and creativity in the arts. In P. Heist (Ed.), *Education for creativity in the American college.* Berkeley: Center for Research and Development in Higher Education, 1966.

GILLESPIE, M. M., & ALLPORT, G. W. *Youth's outlook on the future.* New York: Doubleday, 1955.

GOLDSEN, ROSE, ROSENBERG, M., WILLIAMS, R. M. JR., & SUCHMAN, E. A. *What college students think.* Princeton: Van Nostrand, 1960.

GOUGH, H. G. *California psychological inventory—manual.* Palo Alto, California: Consulting Psychologists Press, 1956.

GOUGH, H. G. Techniques for identifying the creative research scientist. *Journal of Psychology,* 1960, *49,* 87–98.

HEATH, D. *Explorations in maturity.* New York: Appleton-Century-Crofts, 1965.

HEIST, P. R. Talented transients in the college context. In P. Heist (Ed.), *Education for creativity in the American college.* Berkeley: Center for Research and Development in Higher Education, 1966.

HEIST, P. R., MC CONNELL, T. R., MASTLER, F., & WILLIAMS, PHOEBE. Personality and scholarship. *Science,* 1961, *133,* 362–367.

HELSON, RAVENNA. Creativity, sex, and mathematics. In D. W. MacKinnon (Ed.), *The creative person.* Berkeley: Institute of Personality Assessment and Research, 1961.

HELSON, RAVENNA. Personality of women with imaginative and artistic interests: The role of masculinity, originality, and other characteristics in their creativity. *Journal of Personality,* 1966, *34,* 1–25.

JACOB, P. E. *Changing values in college.* New York: Harper, 1957.

KATZ, J. Students and teaching: Proposals for action, assessment, and research. Stanford, California: Institute for the Study of Human Problems, 1965. (Mimeographed.)

KATZ, J., & KORN, H. Research Report I, December, 1963; Research Report II, February, 1964. Stanford, California: Institute for the Study of Human Problems. (Mimeographed.)

KATZ, J., *et al. Psychological development and the impact of the college: Report of the student development study.* Stanford, California: Institute for the Study of Human Problems, 1966. (Mimeographed).

KENISTON, K. *The uncommitted: Alienated youth in American society.* New York: Harcourt, 1965.

KERR, C. The frantic race to remain contemporary. *Daedalus, Fall,* 1964, 1051–1070.

KINSEY, A. C., POMEROY, W. B., & MARTIN, C. W. *Sexual behavior in the human male.* Philadelphia: Saunders, 1951.

KINSEY, A. C., & GEBHARD, P. H. *Sexual behavior in the human female.* Philadelphia: Saunders, 1953.

KNAPP, R. Changing functions of the college professor. In N. Sanford (Ed.), *The American college.* New York: Wiley, 1962.

KUBIE, L. The forgotten man of education. *Harvard Alumni Bulletin,* February 6, 1954.

LIPPITT, R., & WHITE, R. K. The social climate of children's groups. In R. Barker, J. Kounin, & H. F. Wright (Eds.), *Child Behavior and developmenut.* New York: McGraw-Hill, 1943.

MACFARLANE, JEAN. Perspectives on personality consistency and change from the guidance study. *Vita Humana,* 1964, *7,* 115–126.

MACKINNON, D. W. (Ed.). *The creative person.* Berkeley: Institute of Personality Assessment and Research, 1961.

MACKINNON, D. W. The nature and nurture of creative talent. *American Psychologist,* 1962, *17,* 484–485.

MACKINNON, D. W. Education for creativity: A modern myth. In P. Heist (Ed.), *Education for creativity in the American college.*

Berkeley: Center for Research and Development in Higher Education, 1966.

MCCLELLAND, D. C. Encouraging excellence. *Daedalus, Fall,* 1961, 711–724.

MCCLELLAND, D. C., BALDWIN, A. L., BRONFENBRENNER, U., & STRODTBECK, F. L. *Talent and society.* Princeton: Von Nostrand, 1958.

NEWCOMB, T. M. *Personality and social change.* New York: Dryden, 1943.

NEWCOMB, T. M. Student peer-group influence. In N. Sanford (Ed.), *The American college.* New York: Wiley, 1962.

NICHOLS, R. C. Personality change and the college. *National Merit Scholarship Reports,* Vol. 1, No. 2, 1965.

PINNER, F. The crisis of the state universities: Analysis and remedies. In N. Sanford (Ed.), *The American college.* New York: Wiley, 1962.

RIESMAN, D. The uncommitted generation. *Encounter,* 1960, *15,* 25–30.

RIESMAN, D., & JENCKS, C. The viability of the American college. In N. Sanford (Ed.), *The American college.* New York: Wiley, 1962.

ROE, ANNE. A survey of alcohol education in elementary and high schools in the United States. New Haven: *Quarterly Journal of Studies on Alcohol,* 1943, *3,* 574–662.

RUSSELL, R. D. A survey of alcohol education. In *Alcohol education and its implications for the youthful driver: Proceedings of a workshop.* Providence: Rhode Island State Department of Education, 1961.

SANFORD, N. (Ed.). Personality development during the college years. *Journal of Social Issues,* 1956, *12,* 1–71.

SANFORD, N. (Ed.). *The American college.* New York: Wiley, 1962.

SANFORD, N. The freeing and the acting out of impulses in late adolescence. In R. W. White (Ed.), *The study of lives.* New York: Atherton, 1963.

SANFORD, N. *Self and society.* New York: Atherton, 1966.

SKAGER, R., HOLLAND, J. L., & BRASKAMP, L. A. Changes in self-ratings and life goals among students at colleges with different characteristics. *Research reports, No. 14.* Iowa City, Iowa: American College Testing Program, 1966.

SNYDER, B. How fare creative youth in the modern sciences? In P. Heist (Ed.), *Education for creativity in the American college.* Berkeley: Center for Research and Development in Higher Education, 1966.

SOMERS, R. H. The mainsprings of the rebellion: A survey of Berkeley students in November, 1964. In S. M. Lipset & S. S. Wolin, (Eds.). *The Berkeley student revolt.* New York: Doubleday, 1965.

SUCHMAN, E. A. The values of American college students. In A. E. Traxler (ed.), *Long range planning for education.* Washington, D.C.: American Council on Education, 1958.

WATSON, G. What are the effects of democratic atmosphere on children? *Progressive Education,* 1940, *17,* 336–342.

WEBSTER, H., FREEDMAN, M. B., & HEIST, P. Personality changes in college students. In N. Sanford (Ed.), *The American college.* New York: Wiley, 1962.

WHITE, R. W. *Lives in progress.* New York: Holt, 1952.

Acknowledgments

Most of the chapters in *Where Colleges Fail* were written specifically for this book, although some rest heavily on material that I published before. For permission to use my copyrighted material, I want to thank the following: The Stern Family Fund for "Commentary on the Present State of the Art of Recognizing Excellence: Individual Reactions," in *Recognition of Excellence,* 1960; the *Teachers College Record* for "General Education and Personality Theory," 1965, *66,* 721–732; The American Academy of Arts and Sciences for "The Human Problems Institute and General Education," *Daedalus,* Summer, 1965; the Board of Education of the Methodist Church for "Social Change and the College Student" and "The Size of the University and its Implications," Chs. 4 and 5 in W. A. Geier, (Ed.), *Today's Student and his University,* 1966; the University of Oregon Alumni Association for "Student Morality: Prospects for a New Ethic," in *Old Oregon,* September-October, 1966; the McGraw-Hill Book Company for "Implications for Education and for Adjustment of Curricula to Individual Students," in Earl J. McGrath (Ed.), *Universal Higher Education,* 1966; and the Institute of Higher Education, Columbia University, for "The Development of Social Responsibility," in Earl J. McGrath (Ed.), *The Liberal Arts College's Responsibility for the Individual Student,* 1966; and The Association for Childhood Education International for "Dominance versus Autocracy and the Democratic Character, *Childhood Education,* November 1964, Vol. 23, No. 3.

For help of various kinds in the preparation of the manuscript warm thanks go to members of the staff of the Institute for the Study of Human Problems, Stanford University, particularly to Joseph Katz with whom I have discussed all the issues taken up in this book and who gave many valuable criticisms and suggestions. Craig Comstock, Harold Webster, and Patricia Kollings worked with devotion and high competence to make the manuscript readable, and I am deeply in their debt.

NEVITT SANFORD

Stanford, California
January, 1967

A

Index

B